FILM DIRECTING

KILLER STYLE & CUTTING EDGE TECHNIQUE

FILM DIRECTING

KILLER STYLE & CUTTING EDGE TECHNIQUE

RENÉE HARMON

SHREWSBURY COLLEGE
LONDON RD. LRC

lone eagle
PUBLISHING COMPANY

Los Angeles, CA

FILM DIRECTING
Killer Style & Cutting Edge Technique
© 1998 by Renée Harmon. All rights reserved.

LONE EAGLE PUBLISHING CO., LLC™
2337 Roscomare Road, Suite Nine
Los Angeles, CA 90077-1851
Phone: 800-FILMBKS • Toll Free Fax: 888-FILMBKS
www.loneeagle.com & www.eaglei.com

Printed in the United States of America
Cover design by Lindsay Albert

Library of Congress Cataloging-in-Publication Data
Harmon, Renée.
    Film directing—killer style and cutting edge techniques :
a step-by-step guide to making your film / by Renée Harmon.
        p.   cm.
    Includes bibliographical reference and index.
    ISBN 0-943728-89-4
    1. Motion pictures—Production and direction.   I. Title.
PN1995.9.P7H38   1997
791.43'0233—dc21   97-8336
                                                    CIP

CONTENTS

INTRODUCTION, vii

PART 1: THE COLLABORATIVE ART
   1.1 All About Teamwork, 2
   1.2 The Director's Contract, 8

PART 2: THE INTERPRETATION OF THE FILM'S
         EMOTIONAL AND VISUAL THRUST
         Introduction Analysis Of The Script, 10
   2.1 Your Directing Style, 11
   2.2 Impact Of The Environment, 15
   2.3 The Gradation Of Rhythm And Pacing, 17
   2.4 Viewpoint, 27
   2.5 Forward Movement, 35
   2.6 Structure, 39
   2.7 Getting To Know The Characters, 42

PART 3: CREATING THE ON-SCREEN IMAGE
         Introduction, 64
   3.1 Movement, 65
   3.2 Viewpoint, 73
   3.3 Framing, 76
   3.4 Editing, 78
   3.5 Editing Concepts, 85

PART 4: THE ELEMENTS OF SOUND AND LIGHT
   4.1 Sound, Dialogue And Music, 94
   4.2 Lighting, 102

PART 5: THE DIRECTOR AND THE ACTOR

      Introduction, 112

  5.1 The Complex Character And
        The Simple Character, 115

  5.2 The Sensitive Actor And
        The Less Sensitive Actor, 123

  5.3 Dialogue, 135

  5.4 The Director And The "Star," 144

  5.5 The Director And The Casting Process, 146

PART 6: THE DIRECTOR AND THE LOCUSTS
       OF CREATIVITY

  6.1 Avoiding The Locusts, 154

PART 7: THE DIRECTOR'S HOMEWORK

  7.1 The Storyboard, 160

  7.2 More Lists, 167

PART 8: WHAT NOW?

  8.1 Your Road Map To Success, 172

  8.2 The Interviews, 176

  8.3 Information-Achievement Cycle, 181

  8.4 Decisions, 186

CONCLUSION, 188

APPENDICES

      Unions and Guilds, 189
      International Film Commissions, 194

GLOSSARY, 211

BIBLIOGRAPHY, 214

INDEX, 215

ABOUT THE AUTHOR, 221

INTRODUCTION

Film Directing: Killer Style & Cutting Edge Technique has been written for you, the director. Although skilled in basic directing techniques, you may need advice on how to achieve the emotional and visual impact demanded by motion picture audiences today. You may have a clear *vision* about the way a specific moment should be viewed on the screen, but may lack the finer directorial skills necessary to give that vision artistic expression.

The director choreographs actors and camera movements, decides upon the lighting, sound and editing patterns and makes the events on the screen exciting. The director's skill thus directly leads to the viewer's involvement with actions and emotions and helps the viewer identify with events as they unfold on the screen.

Like a stage play, film is the expression of an immense range of human endeavors and emotions but film differs from the stage because at its best, film is more effective in visualizing emotional, social and cultural disturbances and interactions. A motion picture gives an event a sense of realism that surrounds personal experiences and also makes visible the hidden emotions caused by these experiences. In this way, film affects a viewer's response as a stage play won't. During a play, the viewer is part of the audience to whom a story is presented but when watching a film, the viewer becomes *part of the action* on screen.

The director of a play *depicts* a situation for an audience, no matter the size. On the other hand, though a movie theater may be sold out, the film director's work *relates* to one person only . . . the viewer, who, hopefully, identifies with the character, his situations and actions and becomes the hero on the screen. This identification process is why the image of the person on screen has a far greater impact on a viewer than does the live actor on stage.

The viewer's identification with characters or events on screen is the key to a film's appeal and box office success, whether the motion picture is a low-budget independent or a multi-million dollar studio production.

How to create the viewer's identification—the core of all blockbuster movies—is what *Film Directing: Killer Style & Cutting Edge Technique* is all about.

Film Directing: Killer Style & Cutting Edge Technique gives you the "know how" you need to draw the viewer into your story on the screen. In short, *Film Directing: Killer Style & Cutting Edge Technique* places you into the viewer's position.

PART 1

THE
COLLABORATIVE
ART

1.1 All About Teamwork

The poem, the musical composition, the painting—these different forms of art have one thing in common: each is an expression of an individual mind. Not so for the art form known as the film, which demands the cooperation of artists and technicians. Once a production begins principal photography, it is the director's responsibility to complete an artistically and technically sound work, within its allotted time schedule and budget. Though the director needs to keep a tight rein on every aspect of production, he also must get along with all members of his crew.

Years ago, the director's job was simply to direct the picture. A modicum of attention may have been given to the "director's cut" of the film, but basically, the director was hired to direct the screenwriter's script and then to relinquish his responsibility as soon as he ended production by announcing, "That's a wrap!"

Today, the director is involved with a film from the script's first rewrite to the completion of post-production (and sometimes, from the script's inception to its release). This does not mean the director must be an expert in all technical areas of filmmaking; such knowledge, in fact, may backfire if the director becomes a dictator on the set, thus alienating the teammates. However, you should feel strongly about your vision of the film; if you permit others to interfere with your decisions, you'll lose credibility and control. Don't forget: the director has the final say.

And now, let's meet the director's key teammates:
- Producer
- Writer
- Production Manager

- Cinematographer
- Production Designer
- Editor

THE DIRECTOR AND THE PRODUCER

A director's successful collaboration with the producer largely is a matter of appreciating the fact that, without the producer, there would be nothing to direct. The producer is a businessperson: he owns the script; he is in the market to buy the script; or, he hires a writer to develop an idea into a script. Once the script is completed, the producer formulates a budget for it and then tries to interest a major studio or an independent film company in his project. (At this point of the project's development, because the film exists only as a screenplay, distribution companies normally will not commit to distribution; all the producer expects is a "Letter of Intent.") Next, the producer arranges financing of the project via a "Limited Partnership" or an "Investment Contract." Or, if he has an extensive track record of successful films and has a "bankable" actor committed to starring in the film, he'll try for a number of "pre-sales." (The entire financing process could take the producer a few months or several years.)

Finally, the producer puts together his production team, headed by the director. Once the production begins principal photography, the producer turns over the reins to you, the director. Until post-production looms, the producer has to watch proceedings from the wings, checking to make sure that the time schedule and the budget remain on course.

Respect the parameters the producer has provided: do your best to bring in his film on time and on budget.

THE DIRECTOR AND THE WRITER

Ideally, the director would become involved with the script during the final phase of rewriting. Always respect the writer's ideas and his opinion about the story, but let it be known that you know HOW and in what way each story sequence will best project on the screen. (Many writers assume that their eloquent expressions on paper automatically translate to the screen.) It is therefore up to the director to transform the writer's (possibly) vague conceptional details into concrete examples of WHAT, WHY and HOW.

As you work with the writer, be careful about bringing in your own ideas. Suggest changes, explaining why they should be made. But, don't demand and don't try to upstage the writer. Remember: the writer writes and the director directs. If the writer is not open to your suggestions, discuss them with the producer, explaining that your recommendations are in reference to the *logical cinematic interpretation* of events and/or relationships. After all, your job as director is to develop the script's logic within the framework of Motive and Reaction, as well as to ensure the script's visual and emotional aspects.

THE DIRECTOR AND THE PRODUCTION MANAGER

The production manager must keep the production "on track." There is likely to be some friction between the two of you, but try hard to work compatibly with him. Be aware of the thin line between the production manager's budgetary requirements and your artistic demands. To help you understand the production manager's concerns, get involved in the script's schedule breakdown (more about this appears in Part 7, "The Director's Homework").

Be aware of these few caveats to ensure a compatible relationship with the production manager:

- Don't wait until principal photography begins to argue for more shooting days or for better locations. These appeals should be mentioned during the script's breakdown period. Your requests may be granted or, more than likely, you will be asked to keep your schedule and breakdowns within the limits of the allotted time schedule and budget.
- During production, adhere to the time limits on your shot list. Don't waste time setting up or rehearsing. However, don't permit the production manager to rush you during production.

THE DIRECTOR AND THE CINEMATOGRAPHER

The cinematographer (also known as the director of photography, or DP) is the teammate upon whom you'll depend most. Work with, not against, each other. Discuss your vision of the film; he may not visualize it the same way you do. Insist on viewing some of his previous film work. Even if he is an award-winning cinematographer, his techniques may not coincide with your vision. (It's better to find out before he is hired whether or not his style and technique are compatible with your vision.) Realize that the cinematographer most likely will be more concerned about a film's visual effectiveness than either its storyline or character development.

Because you will work very closely with the cinematographer, seriously consider his suggestions in relation to putting your vision onto the screen, but never permit him to become a creative dictator. (Remember, advice is one thing, interference is another.)

Listen to your DP's advice on a location's suitability (one location may be more difficult, and therefore more time-consuming, to light than another). Before the production manager finalizes the shooting schedule, speak to your DP to make sure that the schedule allows him enough time for lighting and camera setup. If possible, collaborate with the cinematographer on the script breakdown.

THE DIRECTOR AND THE PRODUCTION DESIGNER

The production designer (also known as the art director) conceptualizes the director's vision by designing the "look" of the film, including sets and locations. He also must consider the needs of the cinematographer (who lights and photographs the set and/or location); the sound person; and the producer (who tries to keep the film within its budget). As the film's director, you must guide the look and style of the piece, so let your production designer know your vision and insist on being included in the location scouts. (Remember, a room's dimensions will change a scene's staging.)

THE DIRECTOR AND THE EDITOR

Never consider the editor's work mechanical or uncomplicated simply because she works from a completed shooting script. The editor makes an important contribution to the film's creative process. Through her skills, the editor can bring motion and tempo to a dramatic climax that extends beyond the words on the page or the director's visual concept. During the editing process, the editor must consider the viewer's response to the image on the screen. For example, a scene that appeared to be completely sensible during production might be confusing when edited together.

Therefore, DO listen to the advice of your skilled and creative editor. By the time your film goes to the editor, you have worked closely on it for a very long time and it may be difficult for you to view it objectively. So, stand back and let the editor take an unbiased look at your work.

But watch out: the editor has the power to edit your work either into a coherent film or to destroy its congruity. An obstinate editor can harm the film's rhythm, while a creative editor will work diligently on the picture's motive and reaction (cause and effect). Therefore, if possible, get to know the editor who has been assigned to your film and work hard to create a harmonious relationship so that your views on the film are in sync.

1.2 The Director's Contract

The following Director's Guild of America (DGA) basic contract will give you some guidelines on what to expect and what to ask for when signing your deal:

- Depending on the film's budget, the DGA requires that the director be compensated for a minimum number of weeks for his work on pre-production, principal photography and post-production.
- The director's salary must be guaranteed.
- If the film's shooting date is delayed (but not more than six weeks), no additional salary is due to the director.
- If the film is to be canceled, the director's salary must be paid. (This holds true only for DGA members; those not in the guild will likely lose any salary owed them.)
- Twenty percent (20%) of the director's salary will be paid in weekly installments during pre-production; sixty percent (60%) will be paid in weekly installments during principal photography; ten percent (10%) will be paid upon the completion of the director's cut; ten percent (10%) will be paid upon the delivery of the "answer" print.
- Concerning the director's credit, his name must appear on a single card during the film's front titles. His name must appear on all one-sheets and newspaper advertisements. Stipulations require the director's credit to appear last on titles, advertisements and one-sheets.

PART 2

THE INTERPRETATION OF THE FILM'S EMOTIONAL AND VISUAL THRUST

Introduction
Analysis Of The Script

A script, even a well-written one, provides only a film's basic framing—a well-written script does not necessarily make a great film. Therefore, as the director, you must analyze the script thoroughly. You and the writer(s) should discuss the script a number of times. Carefully look at the script's plot and pacing; the characters' goals, obstacles and relationships; you may want to add, cut or rearrange scenes or sequences. When every aspect of the script captures your vision of it, you are ready to translate the script's storyline into cinematic terms—you are ready to write the shooting script.

Because all of the story elements are in place, it's now time to study the script in terms of its emotional and visual value. During this period, you'll make decisions regarding:

- Your Directing Style;
- The Impact of the Film's Environment;
- The Film's Rhythm and Pacing.

2.1 Your Directing Style

When crafting a script's underlying mood, its story is not as important as the director's interpretation of it, which is illustrated by his individual style of directing. Don't confuse the term, "directing style" with camera setups (the scene's staging) or the scene's flow (its movement or choreography). Directing style refers to the *visual technique* selected to symbolize human emotions and actions in the film.

REALISTIC STYLE

Most films (and all television shows and television movies) are directed in the realistic style, which tells a story simply but clearly by presenting an *unbroken illusion of reality*. This style gives the viewer a strong sense of identification as it follows a singular line of visual cause and effect. In a film directed in this style, characters are individualized and emphasis is placed upon the interaction between characters, their strong but everyday logic, and their believable (or, realistic) reaction to each other. Oftentimes, social problems are encountered in films directed in a realistic style.

Visually, the realistic film utilizes an overall monochromatic lighting scheme (i.e., soft lighting); music is used sparingly; sets depict realism; the editor uses the Invisible Editing Style(see 3.5, "Editing Concepts"). Following is an example of a script utilizing the Realistic Style of Directing:

Example

```
EXT.—BUSY DOWNTOWN STREET

On ERIC as he leaves the office building.
Pan with him as he walks down the street to
a parking lot. He looks up.
```

```
ERIC'S POV
High-rises, all a bit old and worn.
On ERIC.
Tired, eager to get home. He walks on.
```

Films directed with Realistic Style include: *Schindler's List* (MCA, 1993, Steven Spielberg, 195 mins.); *Pretty Woman* (Touchstone, 1990, Garry Marshall, 117 mins.).

EPIC STYLE

The epic directing style relies upon the *panoramic use of setting and action*. In this style, emotions are strong and characters and events appear "larger than life." The impressive settings—interior as well as exterior—are also an integral part of the film's visual scope. Conflict, dialogue and action climax in peaks of discordance. Character development is at the core of the epic style, though characters often tend to be clichéd. The director must work hard to endow these larger-than-life characters with human qualities and to depict the actions within a realm of possibility.

Though many high-budget films are directed in the epic style, don't hesitate to use it for your low-budget fantasy or horror film. The emotional and visual thrust of a film directed in this style does not rely on large crowd scenes, special effects or grandiose sets, but rather on the innovative use of light, sound and staging. Following is an example of a script utilizing the Epic Style of Directing:

Example

```
EXT. BUSY DOWNTOWN STREET

On ERIC as he leaves the office building.
Pan with him as he strides down the street—
head held high, his briefcase swinging
aggressively to and fro. He looks up.
```

```
ERIC'S POV.

The high-rises shine like medieval for-
tresses in the late afternoon's sun.

On ERIC.

"A knight in shining armor." He proudly
walks on.
```

Films directed with Epic Style include: *The Deer Hunter* (MCA, 1978, Michael Cimino, 183 mins.); *The Godfather* (Paramount, 1972, Francis Ford Coppola, 171 mins.).

EXPRESSIVE STYLE

The expressive style goes beyond realism by presenting *subjective patterns of realism*—situations and events are not presented to the viewer as they occur, but rather as the character experiences them. This style raises details to allegorical levels by changing the viewer's conventional and habitual notions about situations. In this directing style, a scene is broken into a varied (and at times unrelated) series of shots. Mood, emotion and reaction are often juxtaposed within a single scene.

Successfully employing the expressive style demands close interaction between director and editor. Admittedly, this style does not concentrate on directing but rather on editing, which gives the expressive style its flair. As a result, this style gives the editor a huge field in which to showcase her creativity.

Since this style utilizes symbolism and concentrates on character, an entire film directed this way may confuse the viewer and create boredom. However, the expressive style can cause an impact if used sparingly, within the context of a film directed in the realistic or epic style. Following is an example of a script utilizing the Expressive Style of Directing:

Example

```
EXT. Busy Downtown Street

On ERIC as he leaves the office building.
Pan with him as he walks down the street to
the parking lot. He looks up.

ERIC's POV.

Tilted camera: ZOOM shot of high-rises
tumbling down.

ON ERIC

Medium Long Shot of Eric. He gasps, tenses.

ERIC'S POV.

The buildings recede, then they appear to
advance, and recede again. A high-pitched
SOUND IS HEARD.

Medium Long Shot of Eric staring. Camera
MOVES IN to Tight Medium Shot, Eric protec-
tively covering his head with his hands.
```

Films directed with Expressive Style include: *The Exorcist* (Warner Bros., 1973, William Friedkin, 120 mins.); *Psycho* (MCA, 1960, Alfred Hitchcock, 109 mins); *The Birds* (MCA, 1963, Alfred Hitchcock; 120 mins.).

Regardless which directing style you select for your film, be aware that, at times, dialogue may be secondary to the emotional and visual aspects of the film.

Exercise

Situation: HIKERS are caught in a forest fire and must fight their way out of the woods. Decide which directing style might be most suitable. Then, write a short scenario.

2.2 Impact Of The Environment

Environment is the unifying force that brings the diverse narrative elements together; as a result, it plays a dynamic role in the development of your film's emotional and visual aspects. As the director, you must decide how integral to the film you want the environment to be. Often, it is environment that compels the director to select one directing style over another.

Environment can take on frightening aspects that move characters to *specific actions,* or it can be the unnoticeable background of everyday life. However, showing the viewer a character's *reaction to environment* can explain that character's specific actions. In this respect, characters relate to environment in the same way they relate to the film's other characters: they may or may not be in accord with the environment. In other words, environment and action may be complementary or opposed to each other. Following are examples of complementary environment and action; and environment and action in opposition.

Examples

Complementary Environment and Action

```
INT. SUSIE'S BEDROOM

The bed is unmade, clothes are scattered
all around, unwashed plates litter the
floor.

SUSIE enters. She kicks some jeans and
sweaters out of her way. With a contented
sigh, she collapses on the bed.
```

Environment and Action In Opposition

```
INT. SUSIE'S BEDROOM

The bed is unmade, clothes are scattered
around, unwashed plates litter the floor.
```

MARGE, Susie's mother, enters. She is dressed in a smart business suit and carries a briefcase. She looks at the mess, tense with disbelief. She picks up a dirty dish, places it on the dressing table, reaches for a tissue, then wipes her hands. She shakes her head and exits hastily.

Exercise

RITA and MAX, on a fishing expedition, enter the shack they have rented. Write a shooting script, showing how the characters are either complementary or in opposition to the environment.

Example

INT. SHACK

RITA and MAX enter the shack.

> MAX
> Here we are. Nice place, ain't it.

> RITA
> Perfect.

> MAX
> Not exactly the Ritz, but....

> RITA
> ...we'll manage...somehow.

2.3 The Gradation Of Rhythm And Pacing

The well-crafted film consists of separate shots; when combined into individual scenes, these shots create the film's gradated episodic structure relating to plot, character relationships and visual elements. The most effective way to study your film's gradation pattern is to look carefully at its rhythm and pacing before writing the shooting script. *Rhythm* refers to visual gradation; *pacing* refers to emotional gradation.

Many well-made films lack gradation in these two areas. Then, they appear choppy or monotonous because the majority of scenes operate either on unrelated or identical *Intensity Levels*. In this respect, it doesn't matter whether a film depends mostly on physical action (i.e., the genres of action, fantasy, horror) or upon emotional content (i.e., the genres of drama or comedy). If a film lacks intensity levels (rhythm and pacing), it will feel too static. There are three basic levels of intensity:

- Intensity Level I   =   Low Intensity
- Intensity Level II   =   Medium Intensity
- Intensity Level III   =   High Intensity

Exercises

Write one-page scenarios applying Intensity Levels to the following situations:

Physical Action (Rhythm)
A fist fight.
- Intensity Level I: Toddlers Lou and Mike eye each other's toys.
- Intensity Level II: Lou and Mike grab each other's toys.

- Intensity Level III: Lou and Mike start fighting over the toys.

Visual Aspects (Rhythm)

Hikers on a mountain trail worry about an upcoming storm.

- Intensity Level I: Hikers notice some clouds gathering behind a mountain.
- Intensity Level II: Hikers see clouds blanketing the sky.
- Intensity Level III: Hikers worry because thunder rolls and lightning flashes.

Human Interaction (Pacing)

A married couple plan their vacation.

- Intensity Level I: Lem and Ruth discuss their vacation plans.
- Intensity Level II: Lem and Ruth argue over what to do for their vacation: should they take a cruise to Bermuda or visit Lem's mother in Minnesota.
- Intensity Level III: Ruth accuses Lem of loving his mother more than her; Lem accuses Ruth of foolishly spending his hard-earned money.

Emotions (Pacing)

A woman cleans out her closet and discovers an old treasure.

- Intensity Level I: Searching through some old letters, Laura is pleased to discover a photo of her grandmother.
- Intensity Level II: Happily, Laura recalls the wonderful vacations she used to have on her grandmother's farm.
- Intensity Level III: Laura's tender memories change to grief because her grandmother died

last year. Holding onto the picture, Laura cries bitterly.

CHANGING RHYTHMS

Your film's overall rhythm is decided by *changing the intensity patterns* of scenes. Although some directors like to gradually build intensity levels, the levels do not have to follow the typical I-II-III sequencing. Your film can feature intensity levels in different combinations, for example

- Level I → Level II → Level III
  or,
- Level I → Level III → Level I
  or,
- Level III → Level II → Level I
  or,
- Level II → Level I → Level III

Let's have some fun with different intensity levels.

Example

A group of aliens invades a small town.

Their first stop is the local diner for lunch.

EXT. TOWN *(Intensity Level III)*

A spaceship zooms into town.

INT. DINER *(Intensity Level I)*

Disregarding the lunchtime crowd waiting to be served, three teenage WAITRESSES discuss and giggle about the upcoming prom.

EXT. DINER *(Intensity Level II)*

ALIENS land in front of the diner.

INT. DINER *(Intensity Level I)*

The giggling teenage waitresses rush to the window.

EXT. DINER *(Intensity Level II)*

> The aliens swagger up to the diner.
>
> INT. DINER *(Intensity Level III)*
>
> The aliens burst into the diner. Bedlam.
> Waitresses, CUSTOMERS and OWNER rush
> around, all trying to save themselves.
>
> *(Intensity Level I)* The alien leader,
> flashing a Visa card, humbly asks to be
> seated.

Changing intensity levels keeps the viewer's attention. At times, a film may exhibit well-applied intensity levels within scenes but will miss the overall gradation, resulting in a dull film. Let's take a look at an overall intensity gradation that will maintain the viewer's interest throughout a film:

Act I

The film begins at Intensity Level II, followed by a drop to Intensity Level I, giving the viewer a moment to catch his breath. Act I ends with Intensity Level III (i.e., a plot twist, event or question leading into Act II).

Act II

The film continues in a graduated pattern. Interchange Intensity Levels I and II; every so often, insert a short Intensity Level III scene. Somewhere in the middle of Act II, there should be a featured scene at Intensity Level III. Act II should end with an Intensity Level III sequence (i.e., a dark moment).

Act III

The beginning of Act III should offer a scene dropping the intensity to Level I, but it then should move quickly to the film's denouement, at Intensity Level III. At this point in the script, all loose ends should be tied up. Do not weaken the film by adding more, unnecessary scenes.

Intensity Levels must relate to plot and story content. For example, a burning house is not frightening unless the viewer knows that someone is trapped inside. Or, two cars speeding down a highway do not offer excitement unless one of them has been established as a robber's getaway car. Or, a heart-warming reunion between divorced mother and divorced daughter is not compelling unless the viewer realizes they are in love with the same man. *Scent Of A Woman* (MCA, 1992, Martin Brest, 157 mins.) illustrates an excellent use of different Intensity Levels. Compare this film to *The Pelican Brief* (Warner Bros., 1993, Alan J. Pakula, 141 mins.), which demonstrates a less satisfactory use of Intensity Levels.

PACING

Pacing refers to the *tapestry of human relationships*, the all-important building blocks that provide a film's emotional gradations. Interrelationships give a film its forward thrust. Check pacing patterns thoroughly during your script analysis and stay with your decisions during production. If you don't, you may have terrific-looking dailies, but you might end up with a string of disappointing scenes when the film is edited because you'll see that all those great dailies play on the same emotional level. *Do not let any actor talk you into playing a scene differently from the emotional level you had decided upon!* Unless you stick to your plans, you'll find your film caught in a monotonous trap. What tends to happen is that all scenes will play on too high an emotional level or will appear too casual. If a major star is signed to your film and insists upon playing the character his way, pay heed to his suggestions and agree with some of them. However, during production, insist upon a fair number of takes, then select the one that comes closest to the emotional level you had decided upon during the script analysis phase.

Since a film depends far more on its emotional and visual aspects than on dialogue, a well-graduated pacing pattern will deal with the following relationship elements:

- *Communication Levels*;
- The *Shifting Dominance Pattern* between characters;
- A scene's *Apex*.

COMMUNICATION LEVELS

As in rhythm and pacing, communication operates on three levels:

- Communication Level I   = To Explain
- Communication Level II   = To Make a Point
- Communication Level III = To Force the Point

Communication Levels may either portray positive or negative responses.

Without our awareness, we use Communication Levels everyday. In a typical conversation between women discussing an upcoming clothing sale, one might first EXPLAIN why she in interested in attending; then she would POINT OUT the huge bargains the store will have; if the second woman is still not interested in going, the first woman would then FORCE HER POINT, trying to convince her to go.

Or, do you remember when, as a child, your mom desperately tried to make you eat your vegetables? Does the following scene sound familiar?

Example

Communication Level I: To Explain

MOM

Come on, eat your spinach. It looks yummy. Nice and green. Spinach is good for you. It makes you grow strong and tall.

Communication Level II: To Make a Point

MOM

```
Your brother always eats his spinach. He
never makes a fuss. And he's much younger
than you.
```

Communication Level III: To Force the Point

MOM

```
If you don't eat your spinach right now,
you won't go to Disneyland on Sunday with
the rest of us. And I mean it.
```

Neither an actor's top interpretation of a role, nor your most innovative direction of the scene will maintain the energy in a long dialogue scene and / or narrative, unless—regardless of the written lines—you build the scene and / or narrative via Communication Levels.

SHIFTING DOMINANCE PATTERN

This term refers to the *character dynamics* in a scene, or which character is the "high person" and which is the "low person" in the depicted relationship. For example:

- Joe is the high person at the beginning of the scene; Bill is the low person.
- An apex occurs—both men operate from identical power.
- Joe is the low person at the end of the scene.

APEX

Every well-defined and smoothly running scene includes an apex: the moment when both or all partners operate from the *same emotional and/or intellectual power level*. The apex is the moment of suspense when the viewer wonders who will win in the end.

Inherently combining the Shifting Dominance Pattern, Communication Levels and Apex in lengthy dialogue scenes demands the director's *precise visual interpretation*. But be careful: whether or not the Shifting Dominance and the Apex are emotionally effective depends upon the viewer's interpretation of the scene, or, the scene's visual presentation. To make entertaining a long, potentially dull but necessary scene relies upon your actors' acting skills and also on your choreographing skills. Camera setups and movements must clearly indicate each character's momentary dominance position. For excellent examples of shifting dominance patterns, carefully watch *Midnight Cowboy* (MGM, 1969, John Schlesinger, 113 mins.) or *Dog Day Afternoon* (Warner Bros., 1975, Sidney Lumet, 124 mins.).

<u>Example</u>

The following scene illustrates the elements of Shifting Dominance and Apex.

INT. THE SMITH'S KITCHEN

ALVA and BEN, a middle-aged couple, have finished their dinner. (*Alva—High Man; Ben— Low Man*) Peeling an apple, Ben avoids Alva's questioning look. Alva fiddles with her napkin, pushes her plate back and forth. It is obvious she has something on her mind.

ALVA
How was your day?

BEN
What do you think? I went to the office, shuffled papers...

ALVA
...tried to look busy...

                    BEN
         Yeah. Got to make a
         living. Pay bills.

                    ALVA
         About bills...

                    BEN
         Yeah?

                    ALVA
         There's a charge from
         Russell's Department
         Store. Came in today's
         mail.

                    BEN
              (gets up)
         I better take the dog for
         a walk.

                    ALVA
         You stay right here.

                    BEN
         What's all the fuss
         about? You must've
         charged something.

(*Ben—High Man; Alva—Low Man*)

                    ALVA
         I haven't got a charge
         account at Russell's. You
         charged something... a
         ring...a diamond and ruby
         ring.

                    BEN
         A little something for
         your birthday.

Alva's throat is tight with tears.

                    ALVA
         My birthday was two weeks
         ago. You didn't even give
         me a card.

(*Apex*)

Ben sits next to Alva. He reaches for her
hand.

```
                    BEN
          I'm sorry...Well...I
          didn't buy the ring for
          you...

                    ALVA
          There's...?
```

Ben nods.

```
                    ALVA
               (cont'd)
          Another woman.

                    BEN
          There's been one for some
          time. Now you know. We've
          got to talk. Things
          haven't been too good
          between us lately and I
          met this girl...
```

Exercise

Using the same scene, switch dominance positions.

2.4 Viewpoint

In filmic terms, *viewpoint* is defined as the position the director wishes the VIEWER to take. For example:

- The *Subjective Viewpoint* is when the *viewer identifies with the hero* (i.e., the viewer steps into the hero's "shoes");
- The *Omnipotent (or, Shifting) Viewpoint* occurs when the *viewer is placed in an omnipotent,* or Godlike *position.*

Most likely, you won't make a decision about your film's viewpoint until you write the shooting script. Therefore, it is advantageous to give this topic some thought during the script's analysis phase.

THE SUBJECTIVE VIEWPOINT

When using the Subjective Viewpoint, you put the viewer into the protagonist's "shoes," he becomes part of the hero's problems and/or successes. Therefore, make sure you show ONLY what the hero sees and experiences.

THE OMNIPOTENT (SHIFTING) VIEWPOINT.

In some situations, the Omnipotent Viewpoint can raise a scene's level of suspense, thereby permitting the viewer to experience an event from two different points of view: that of the hero and that of another character.

The following sample scenes illustrate different viewpoints.

Examples

Situation: Beth, a teenage baby-sitter, receives a threatening phone call. She tries to call her employers and her parents but no one is reachable. She calls 911.

Subjective Viewpoint

INT. THE MILLERS' KITCHEN—NIGHT

On BETH. She picks up the phone to call 911. Her finger is on the button when she HEARS footsteps approaching the house. Tensely, she turns to the window.

BETH'S POV

The curtained kitchen window.

BACK TO BETH

Quickly, she puts the receiver down. Pan with her as she tiptoes to the window. DOLLY in to tight MEDIUM SHOT. Beth makes sure the window is closed. Finding it locked, she relaxes a bit.

Pan with Beth as she hurries back to the phone. She picks up the receiver and suddenly flinches.

BETH'S POV

The patio door stands slightly ajar.

Omnipotent Viewpoint

INT. THE MILLERS' KITCHEN—NIGHT

On BETH. She picks up the phone to call 911. Her finger is on the button when she HEARS footsteps approaching the house. Tensely, she turns to the window.

BETH'S POV

The curtained kitchen window.

EXT. THE MILLERS' HOUSE—NIGHT

A hooded FIGURE hides next to the window.

INT. THE MILLERS' HOUSE—NIGHT

Tensely, BETH puts the receiver down. Pan with her as she tiptoes to the window. DOLLY in to tight MEDIUM SHOT.

Beth tries to open the window.

```
EXT. THE MILLERS' HOUSE—NIGHT

The hooded figure crouches down, pulls out
a knife.

INT. THE MILLERS' HOUSE—NIGHT

On Beth. Finding the window locked, she
relaxes a bit. Pan with Beth as she walks
back to the phone.

EXT. THE MILLERS' HOUSE—NIGHT

Pan with the hooded figure as he makes his
way to the patio.

INT. THE MILLERS' HOUSE—NIGHT

Beth picks up the receiver. She dials, then
flinches.

BETH'S POV

The patio door stands slightly ajar.
```

Exercise

Situation: Bookkeeper CHARLES has been embezzling money and is worried about covering up his crime. One morning, at work, his BOSS enters, accompanied by a STRANGER (possibly a police detective). Write a scenario and three shooting scripts . . .

- From the Subjective Viewpoint (Charles' point of view);
- From the Subjective Viewpoint (the detective's point of view);
- From the Omnipotent Viewpoint.

The next step in presenting the viewpoint is to emphasize one element over another by deciding what element you wish to stress in any particular scene or sequence of scenes. There are three elements to consider:

- a *Visual* Emphasis;
- an *Emotional* Emphasis; or
- a *Physical* Emphasis (i.e., action or dialogue).

It is unwise to place two highly emotional scenes next to each other. A better choice is to have a scene with an emotional emphasis followed by one with either visual or physical emphasis.

Example

Visual Emphasis
Situation: Jane breaks up with Sam on Prom Night.

INT. BALLROOM—NIGHT

It's Prom Night. COUPLES are dancing, laughing, flirting; everyone is having a good time.

HOLD ON SAM and JANE.

          SAM
So...you've made up your mind...

          JANE
Of course, I've made up my mind...

CUT TO dancing couples.

          JANE
       (VO)
...I'm going away to college.

BACK TO Sam and Jane.

          SAM
We can still get engaged.

          JANE
Get engaged?

Jane smiles at him. CAMERA FAVORS couples dancing by.

DOLLY IN on Jane and Sam.

          JANE
     (cont'd)
We've talked about it ...kinda.

> SAM
> We said we were going to
> get engaged.
>
> JANE
> I changed my mind. Look,
> I don't want to get
> engaged right now. I
> mean, I'm going to col-
> lege and I'd like to date
> other guys.

Jane lets go of Sam. Pan with her as she
walks through the dancing crowd.

Exercise

Round up a few friends and choreograph the above
scene.

Example

Emotional Emphasis

INT. BALLROOM—NIGHT

It's Prom Night. COUPLES are dancing,
laughing, flirting; everyone is having a
good time.

HOLD ON Sam and Jane.

> SAM
> So...you've made up your
> mind...
>
> JANE
> Of course, I've made up
> my mind.

She snuggles close to Sam.

> JANE
> (cont'd)
> I'm going away to col-
> lege.
>
> SAM
> We can still get engaged.

He kisses her. A loving, passionate kiss.

PULL IN on Sam and Jane.

> JANE
> Get engaged... yeah...we
> talked about it...

ON SAM

> JANE
> (VO)
> ...kind of.

> SAM
> (tensely)
> We said we were going to
> get engaged.

BACK TO Jane and Sam.

> JANE
> I changed my mind. Look,
> I don't want to get
> engaged right now. I
> mean...

SAM'S POV

Jane's face suddenly dims from his vision.
Her voice comes from far away.

> JANE
> (cont'd)
> I'm going away to college
> and I want to date other
> guys.

Exercise

Shoot the scene above with your own video camera.

Example

Physical Emphasis

INT. BALLROOM—NIGHT

It's Prom Night. COUPLES are dancing,
laughing, flirting; everyone is having a
good time.

SAM and JANE dance into the frame. DOLLY IN
on them and HOLD.

> SAM
> So...you've made up your
> mind.

Jane smiles at Sam. A quick turn lands her
tightly in her arms.

> JANE
> I'm going away to col-
> lege.

> SAM
> I know, but we still...

Letting go of Sam, Jane does a few quick
turns.

> JANE
> Get engaged? We talked
> about this.

> SAM
> We said...

ON JANE as she teasingly dances away from
Sam.

> SAM
> (cont'd)
> (VO)
> ...we were going to
> get...

Sam enters frame.

> SAM
> (cont'd)
> ...engaged.

Sam catches up with Jane. He holds her
tightly.

> JANE
> I changed my mind. Look,
> I don't want to get
> engaged right now. I
> mean, I want to go to
> college...

```
Jane struggles free. Pan with her as she
walks off.
                      JANE
                    (cont'd)
              ...and date other guys.
```

Exercise

Design a light plot for the scene above.

2.5 Forward Movement

Every scene in a screenplay—whether characters speak dialogue or are involved in physical action—must move the story forward. When analyzing your script, check it for these elements of *Forward Movement*:

- Need;
- Conflict;
- Suspense (a question raised or answered at the conclusion of most scenes).

NEED

Need is defined as the *character's subconscious desires* and, as such, its importance is greater than a character's motivation and/or subsequent goal. To be believable, Need must reflect an established trait of one of the characters.

> Example
>
> *Situation*: Louise, a college student and struggling actress, is determined to play the lead in a college stage production. Even though her best friend Marcia has won the role, Louise wants to snatch the part for herself.

Louise's behavior might be based on one of her following traits:

- Falsehood. Louise is not after the role, but rather, she wants Marcia's boyfriend (her NEED), who has won the leading male role. Performing with him, Louise hopes to steal the man away from Marcia.
- Low Self-Esteem. Louise hopes that people will notice and accept her (her NEED) once they see her on stage.

- Determination. Serious about her acting career, Louise hopes to convince a theatrical agent to represent her (her NEED).

CONFLICT

There is no forward movement without Conflict. In addition, a film lacks suspense without it and runs the risk of being dull. Conflict may be a matter of life and death (i.e., a situation of tremendous consequence); or, it may relate to an everyday tribulation (minor enough to appear comical).

Though issues may be different, today's pattern of Conflict is still based on the formula invented by Greek writers from centuries past, such as:
- Man versus Man (*Gettysburg*);
- Man versus Nature (*Twister*);
- Man versus Himself (*Dead Man Walking*).

When analyzing your script, make certain that conflict is based on an incident that occurs prior to the beginning of the film's narrative or is connected to the twist (see 2.6, "Structure") that sends the plot into action.

Examples of the *Man versus Man conflict* include:
- Union and Rebel fighting (and dying) at Gettysburg.
- A worker arguing with a co-worker.
- A movie star refusing to return to the set until her demands are met.

Examples of the *Man versus Nature conflict* include:
- Shipwrecked sailors huddling in a lifeboat.
- Mountain climbers, near the top of the Matterhorn, running into unexpected fog.
- A scatterbrained man, on his way to pick up his blind date, realizing he doesn't have her address. He stops to call her but has no coins. On his way to the corner store for change, a stray dog attacks him, ripping his trousers.

Examples of the *Man versus Himself conflict* include:

- James, unhappily married for twenty years, meeting and falling in love with another woman. Deeply religious, he is torn between true love and his religious convictions.
- For years, Betty saves $50 each week for a cruise she longs to take. On her way to the bank to deposit her $50, she sees a beautiful dress on sale. Is she going straight to the bank to deposit her money or is she going to buy the dress?
- Agnes is on a diet and craves snacks. Is she going to sneak a candy bar to satisfy this craving?

SUSPENSE

Contrary to popular belief, suspense is not the prerequisite for mystery, action or horror genres. Nor does it pertain to fights, car chases or ghostly appearances. No matter what genre your film falls into, suspense is defined by the following questions in the viewer's mind:

- What will happen next?
- Why will it happen?
- How will it happen?

When analyzing your script, check carefully for *interconnected suspense patterns*. For example, do not have "Question A," introduced in Scene 1, to be answered in Scene 2. Instead, give the viewer time to stew, making certain that "Question B" has been introduced before "Question A" is answered.

Examples

Question A, Scene 1: Edith and Frank worry about Frank getting accepted to law school. If Scene 1 ends with Frank receiving the letter of acceptance, there is NO SUSPENSE.

Scene 2: Frank meets with his career placement counselor, learning that he might have failed his LAST (the entrance exam for law school). SUSPENSE FROM "QUESTION A" IS INTENSIFIED.

Question B, Scene 3: Frank tries arranging a loan to finance his education and runs into difficulties. This would be INTERLOCKING SUSPENSE.

Scene 4: Discouraged by the loan difficulties, Frank goes home to find a letter of acceptance has arrived.

In this sequence of four scenes, "Question A" has been answered while the answer to "Question B" is pending.

As you can tell. It is Interlocking Suspense that keeps the viewer glued to the screen.

2.6 Structure

Many writers and directors contend that adherence to a script's structure, or its *overall interest buildup,* places them into a "creative straitjacket." This might be true in some cases but think of the films that impressed you, that made you want to become a director. It's likely that most of these were blessed with a workable script structure.

Let's take a look at typical script structure:

ACT I

The first act should last approximately fifteen minutes on film and should concentrate on the following:

- *Where: place and time.* Check to see if the environment, if important to the story, has been established sufficiently.
- *WHO: main characters.* Introduce all main characters in this act. If a main character is introduced in Act II, there should be a logical (and good) reason. However, avoid introducing all the main characters at the same time (e.g., at a party).
- *WHAT: main plot.* The plot, which should contain the film's *line of action,* determines the film's directing style.
- *WHAT: subplot,* or the film's *secondary line of action.* A film emphasizing action uses the subplot to reveal relationships between main characters. A film based on relationships and / or social issues uses the subplot to clarify its theme.
- *PROTAGONIST'S MAIN GOAL.* The hero's need (based on one of his traits) forces him into action.
- *ANTAGONIST'S MAIN GOAL.* The villain might be

another character(s), nature or the hero's inner conflict about an issue or person.

- *TWIST.* At the end of Act I, this twist should alter an existing condition and force the hero into action. If the twist is based on conflict, make certain the root of conflict is connected to an incident that occurred prior to Act I (the script's *"back story"*). If the twist is related to an event, be sure it is of grave personal importance to the hero.

ACT II

The second act should last approximately eighty-five minutes on film. It should be filled with suspenseful events. No matter how compelling or gripping the basic plot of the movie is, if the director fails to keep the viewer's interest, it will meander to a denouement in which no one will be interested. Therefore, concentration on the following points is recommended:

- Keep the viewer's interest via suspenseful moments, such as questions which need answers. Remember to utilize the *interconnected suspense patterns* (see 2.5, "Forward Movement"). For Example
- Pose "Question A" in Scene 3;
- Pose "Question B" in Scene 4 or 5;
- Answer "Question A" in Scene 5 (never answer a question in the scene immediately following that in which it was asked);
- Add a main plot twist that forces events into a new, unsuspecting direction. This twist should occur about one-third of the way into Act II. Follow this with a subplot twist;
- Approximately fifteen minutes into Act II (or, at a point when events threaten to drag), feature a main

plot Highlight Sequence. Follow this with a shorter subplot Highlight Sequence. However, the subplot Highlight Sequence should not stray too far from the story's structure.

Act II should end with a main plot twist (i.e., a dark moment when everything seems lost); this should lead directly to Act III.

ACT III

This act should take approximately twenty minutes on film and should feature the following elements:

- The film's *climax*, or increased tribulations set up during the dark moment. During the climax, events should become more puzzling, dangerous and hopeless.
- The climax should lead directly to the film's *denouement*, or, the answer to the main plot question that had been asked in Act I.

And now a word of warning: If the script you are directing has an exciting story but lacks structure, insist on a rewrite. Take a look at *Bonfire Of The Vanities* (Warner Bros., 1990, Brian DePalma, 126 mins.). This film was based on an excellent novel; it was well-directed; it had a great cast; it featured exciting incidents. However, the film was a critical disappointment because of its lack of script structure.

2.7 Getting To Know The Characters

While analyzing the script, you most likely formed a mental image of the characters populating it. You have read their dialogue, you understand how they feel and why they perform certain actions. In fact, you are convinced you know everything about the script's characters and you're ready to cast. You feel that, when portrayed by skilled actors, the characters on the page will transform into "flesh and blood" people.

Wait. How well do you really know the characters? What do you know about their backgrounds? What were they like as children? Did you figure out what makes them tick? Now is a good time to go back to the script.

During the script analysis phase, you were concerned about structure and visual aspects; you worked on the apex and on relationship dominance; you made sure rhythm and pacing were in place. But, did you take the time to search for hidden human qualities in the characters, or did you look upon them simply as chess pieces to be moved at your will, in order to create the foundation for the emotional-visual patterns necessary to the film?

Though you may feel you know these characters implicitly, casting the roles now may lead to uninspired choices. Subconsciously, you may have created a biased vision of your cast, how they should look and behave. Therefore, if you don't know your characters implicitly before you cast them, your casting selections may consist of actors portraying cardboard characters.

Step back. Get to know your characters by way of *Facts* and *Assumptions*.

FACTS AND ASSUMPTIONS

First of all, approach any character as if you never have met him before. Regardless how difficult it seems, refrain from jumping to any conclusions about this character. Instead, list facts about him, as given in the script:

- What does the character do?
- What does the character say about himself?
- What do others say about him?

After answering these questions, you might be surprised at how incorrect your initial assumptions were and how different the character is from the way you had originally pictured him.

Example

Situation: Joe is convicted of bigamy. In fact, there is a remote possibility that he has killed one of his wives. In this scene, he explains to Marla, his defense attorney, his technique of "attracting broads."

```
            JOE
Things take time...do
whatever it takes...find
out what the broad wants
...is it romance...sex...
companionship, or the
idea she'd finally nailed
a guy who'll bring home
the bacon.

            MARLA
You project whatever the
victim —

            JOE
Hey, Mouthpiece, show a
little respect. Don't
call my adored wives
victims.
```

43

                        MARLA
            YOU didn't show any
            respect. You called your
            wives broads.

                        JOE
            Sorry, just slipped out.
            Didn't wanna be disre-
            spectful to my.... (an
            enchanting grin)
            ...beloved ones.

Leaning back, he eyes Marla from head to
toe. All of a sudden, she is uneasy. She
buttons her sweater to her chin. She puts
on her glasses and looks down at Joe's
file. His smile broadens.

                        JOE
                     (cont'd)
            Nah. Let's call them
            "business associates."
            Kind souls who invested
            in my...ventures.

Marla keeps her eyes on the file.

                        MARLA
            You call your Mercedes,
            your penthouse, your
            Armani suits...

Having gotten a hold of herself, Marla
unflinchingly locks eyes with Joe.

                        MARLA
                     (cont'd)
            ..."business ventures?"

                        JOE
                     (shrugs)
            Right on. Props. All
            necessary to creating a
            certain...atmosphere of
            confidence...credibility.
            The business base, if you
            understand what I mean.

Taking notes, Marla nods.

                    JOE
              (cont'd)
          I find out what they
          want, romance...

                    MARLA
          You've told me that
          already.

                    JOE
          I help them. They help
          me.

                    MARLA
          By investing in your
          "ventures?"

                    JOE
          'Course not. You think
          I'm stupid? First, I
          marry the gal, then I
          admit I'm low on cash
          flow, have to make pay-
          ments to keep my invest-
          ments going...I get the
          money...

                    MARLA
          ...And go on to the next
          one.

                    JOE
          Why not? They all dream
          of magic. Of their one
          and only who comes bear-
          ing gifts: the gold of
          love, the incense of
          admiration that makes
          even the old and ugly
          ones beautiful.

                    MARLA
          And you are that magi-
          cian?

                    JOE
          Yep.

                    MARLA
          I talked to Dr. Goodman.

```
                    JOE
          The shrink.

                   MARLA
          Dr. Goodman is a re-
          spected psychologist.

                    JOE
          A dud, if you ask me.

                   MARLA
          I didn't ask you.
               (beat)
          Dr. Goodman told me
          you're less interested in
          the money than in the
          control you exercise over
          the women you marry.

                    JOE
          Give me a break. I gave
          them the world. I gave
          them what they wanted.
          They loved me. Do you
          hear...

          Joe leaps up and yells at Marla in a
          threatening manner.

                    JOE
                 (cont'd)
          ...I made them happy.
```

ANALYZING THE CHARACTERS

At first glance, Joe appears to be the typical con artist who uses charm, good looks and an easy manner to attract and then cheat women. But once we compare given *Facts* with *Assumptions*, the characterization may change. (Based on life experience and individual personality, each director may arrive at somewhat different conclusions.)

Table 1

FACTS	ASSUMPTIONS
WHAT DOES THE CHARACTER (JOE) DO	
He eyes Marla.	He is a seducer.
He makes Marla uneasy.	He enjoys her uneasiness. He has a mean streak.
Threateningly he leans over Marla.	He exhibits possible psychopathic tendencies.
He calls Marla a "mouthpiece."	He has no respect for her.
WHAT DOES THE CHARACTER SAY ABOUT HIMSELF	
"I find out what the broad wants."	The term "broad" indicates he has little respect for women.
"I deliver the goods."	He is proud of his ability to deliver whatever is desired.
"Let's call them business associates"	Bigamy is business.
"They all dream of magic . . ."	He sees himself as a magician.
"I make women feel desirable"	He is doing a good deed.
"I bring the gift of love and the incense of admiration.	Same as above.
"I am a magician."	He either honestly believes in his magic powers, or Joe the cynic, makes fun of himself and his "trade."
WHAT OTHERS SAY ABOUT THE CHARACTER (JOE)	
Dr. Goodman states Joe is less interested in money than the control he exercises over woman.	Control addict?

After comparing facts and assumptions, and depending on the script's plotline, the director may arrive at the following character composite:

- Joe is an extrovert.
- Joe has a high opinion of himself.

- Filled with charm, seducing women comes as second nature to Joe.
- Joe likes the finer things in life.
- In all likelihood, Joe is amoral and cannot distinguish between right and wrong.
- Joe sees himself as a true magician and, possibly, he sincerely believes in his magical powers.
- Joe has psychopathic tendencies.

FLAT CHARACTER

Episodic (or, day) players, such as a Doorman, a Taxi Driver, a Sales Clerk are defined as *Flat Characters*. If you flesh out a flat character by giving him a few attributes, you will be stripping emphasis away from the main characters.

SIMPLE OR COMPLEX CHARACTERS

Usually, a character is defined as *simple* or *complex* depending upon the director's vision of the characters in relation to the plot and other characters. It does not matter whether or not the character is cast with a lead actor.

When creating Simple or Complex Characters, the director should concentrate on the following elements:

For Simple Characters

- Lineament (posture, build, facial expression);
- Age;
- Occupation, Education, Social Position;
- Health;
- Dominant Character Trait;
- Complementary Character Trait.

For Complex Characters

- Lineament (posture, build, facial expression);
- Age;

- Occupation, Education, Social Position;
- Health;
- Dominant Character Trait;
- Complementary Secondary Character Trait;
- Contradictory Character Trait.

THE SIMPLE CHARACTER—DEFINED

Comedy, musical, action and horror films rely on strong Simple Characters. At times, it will be best to cast an actor who "looks the part." Other times, will be best to ignore lineament in favor of acting skill. In any event, be sure to give the Simple Character a compelling *dominant trait* (NOT a contradictory one) driving him to action. However, any Simple Character will be more interesting should the writer add a *complementary quality* to his dominant trait. A Simple Character comes across successfully if his dominant trait fuses with the actor's own personality.

Example

Rita is a typical Simple Character. Determined to move up, Rita performs her job as best she can. She is happily married and loyal to her husband, family and employer.

Lineament: Rita is attractive, has an erect posture and always wears a friendly smile.

Age: She is in her early thirties.

Occupation: Rita is a policewoman.

Health: Rita is in good health.

Dominant Character Trait: Rita's determination.

Complementary Character Trait: Rita's loyalty.

Study the following films for examples of well-developed Simple Characters: *Breakfast At Tiffany's* (Paramount, 1961, Blake Edwards, 114 mins.); *Goldeneye*

(MGM, 1995, Martin Campbell, 130 mins.); *Grumpy Old Men* (Warner Bros., 1993, Donald Petrie, 104 mins.); *The Sound Of Music* (Twentieth Century-Fox, 1965, Robert Wise, 174 mins.).

THE COMPLEX CHARACTER—DEFINED

If your film offers opaque relationships, mental-emotional and/or social issues, the Complex Character is a better option. Lineament is far less important for the Complex Character than it is for the Simple Character. In addition, contradictory character traits make the Complex Character a challenge for both actor and director.

Example

Let's take another look at Rita, now a Complex Character:

Lineament: At times, Rita's erect posture seems forced and her friendly smile appears phony.

Age: Rita is in her early thirties.

Occupation: Rita is a policewoman. She likes her job, its fringe benefits, the pay and most of her colleagues. But, she is tired of facing crime everyday. Education: Rita holds a B.S. in Education. However, her college days seem far behind her.

Health: Rita suffers from migraine headaches.

Dominant Character Trait: Rita's determination. On one hand, she wants a promotion to detective. On the other hand, she considers changing careers and becoming a teacher. Working on her M.A., she attends night classes at the local university.

Complementary Character Trait: This trait is her loyalty, which is put to the test by irregular working hours and evening college classes, both of which take her away from her family. Worse, when she is at home, she is tired and unenergetic around her husband and children. Therefore, Rita's loyalty is torn between love for her family, her sense of familial responsibility and her strong drive to improve her life (remember, her Dominant Character Trait is determination).

Contradictory Character Trait: Rita's low self-esteem. Her determination (need) to advance in either her job (policewoman) or in her desired vocation (teacher) is based on her low self-esteem: she cannot accept herself as she is. Instead, she must be SOMEONE.

Complementary Contradictory Character Trait: Since the Complex Character is less predictable than the Simple Character, the director must have a concise idea about how the mind of this character works. The skilled director connects a character's goals with his traits by asking:

What (Action), i.e., *What is the character doing?*
Why (Volition), i.e., *Why is the character doing it?*
How (Adaptability), i.e., *How is the character doing it?*

These questions should be asked of every Complex Character because what may be a logical solution for one person—a way of solving a problem or making a decision—will be completely illogical to another.

Example

Situation: Three tortured husbands, Mike, Ralph and Bob, have decided to leave (*WHAT*) their difficult wives (*WHY*). *HOW* each achieves this goal depends upon their individual character traits.

Mike hires an attorney and gets a divorce. *Mike's Traits*: Determination, responsibility.

Ralph packs his golf clubs and a few poetry books. Leaving the house in dire need of repair and his wife with a meager bank account and debt, he drives off to search for "greener pastures." *Ralph's Traits*: Immaturity, irresponsibility.

Bob takes months to design an elaborate escape plan. For example, he takes a second mortgage on their home and opens a separate (personal) account with the money; he obtains a new identity via a fake Social Security card and a fake driver's license. On the planned day, he closes out the bank account and escapes to the Bahamas. *Bob's Traits*: Determination, deviousness.

It is the character's *decision* (*why*) that leads him to physical action or interconnected actions, or to *events* (*what*) executed in a particular way (*how*).

A creative director will make the character's initial moment of decision subtly significant. For example, he may have the character execute a physical action; however, the viewer may not be aware of the action's significance until later.

Most scripts do not pay concise attention to the *moment of decision*; usually scripts provide only clues. At times, it becomes the director's responsibility to develop a seemingly uninteresting character into a complex one. The skilled screenwriter, understanding and respecting the director's creative contributions, often leaves it up to the director to develop and highlight character traits. However, don't be tempted into changing an obvious and compelling Simple Character into a Complex one. If you do, you may misdirect your film's narrative.

Example

Situation: Your film takes place in a country inn. The owner is an old man and he is hiding a secret.

You could make the old man a *Simple Character*.

The busboy is a college kid working at the inn for the summer. He appears only a few times. You could make him "the mystery man" by giving him contradictory traits common to a *Complex Character*.

If the busboy is the one who commits the story's unsolvable crime, the assignment of Simple/Complex Characters (owner/busboy, respectively) would work well.

Exercise

- Analyze the characters of Ben and Alva (from 2.3, "Shifting Dominance Pattern"), looking specifically at Facts and logical Assumptions.
- Once you have a clear image of Ben and Alva, decide whether they are:
    Flat;
    Simple; or
    Complex.

Examples

Situation. Mike and Becky argue about her disastrous spending habits. The script reads:

```
INT. KITCHEN—DAY

Mike looks at the stack of bills on the
kitchen table.

CUT TO Becky, doing the dishes.

BACK TO Mike, who takes another look at the
bills and sighs.
```

The physical action presented in this scene cries out to be made more specific. Here, it is important to remember that a Simple Character's actions—mental and physical—spring from his dominant trait and/or his complimentary trait. If the character is Complex, the actions will be dictated by his Dominant traits and Contradictory traits.

Following are examples on how a director may interpret the actions of the three husbands (Mike, Ralph and Bob) who are leaving their wives:

Mike's Actions

```
INT. KITCHEN—DAY

Mike looks at the stack of bills on the
kitchen table. He sighs, looks up. A long
ponderous look.

CUT TO Becky, doing the dishes.

BACK TO Mike. Slowly, he arranges the bills
into neat piles.
```

Mike's Traits: Orderliness, loyalty.

Ralph's Actions

```
INT. KITCHEN—DAY

Ralph looks at the stack of bills on the
kitchen table. Casually, head tilted a bit,
he looks up at his wife.

CUT TO Irene, doing the dishes.

BACK TO Ralph. He pushes the bills aside,
shrugs, gets up and ambles off.
```

Ralph's Traits: Immaturity, irresponsibility.

Bob's Actions

```
INT. KITCHEN—DAY

Bob sees the stack of bills on the kitchen
table. He looks up and sees
```

```
CUT TO Abby doing the dishes.

BACK TO Bob. A teasing smile comes over his
face. He caresses the bills. After a while,
he looks up again.

CUT TO Abby as she throws pots and Pans
into the sink.

BACK TO Bob. His smile grows wider as he
pushes the bills onto the floor. Chuckling
to himself, he leans way back in his chair.
```

Bob's Traits: Determination, deviousness.

At times, a contradictory character trait (i.e., amorality) may overshadow a dominant character trait (i.e., loving warmth). Such a momentary imbalance of traits offers the viewer an intimate knowledge of that particular character.

<u>Example</u>

Howie—a mob hitman by day, who is used to murdering people in cold blood—is a loving father and husband by night.

Or, a dominant character trait combined with a contradictory character trait creates interesting inner conflict.

<u>Example</u>

Over the years, Courtney has saved for a downpayment on a house. At the moment she is ready to purchase a model home, the stingy side of her nature keeps her from giving up her savings.
Courtney's Dominant Trait: Desire to get ahead.
Courtney's Contradictory Trait: Low self-esteem.

Placing a character's dominant trait in conflict with his complementary trait creates an even more gripping persona because suspense builds when opposing character traits are given equal strength.

<u>Example</u>

Matthew, a pediatrician has worked for years at the only hospital operating in a small town. He dreams of joining a group of physicians taking care of children in Third World countries. Considering the responsibility to his family, he never makes the move.

Matthew's Dominant Trait: Giving love.

Matthew's Complimentary Trait: Sense of responsibility.

<u>Exercise</u>

• Reread one of your favorite novels. Select three characters: a Flat Character, a Simple Character and a Complex character. Write a list of traits for each one.

Study the following films for examples of Complex Characters: *The English Patient* (Miramax Films, 1996, Anthony Manghella); *Dead Man Walking* (Gramercy Pictures, 1995, Tim Robbins); *Schindler's List* (Universal, 1993, Steven Spielberg).

SECONDARY SENSE OF BEING

By sorting out Flat, Simple and Complex characters, you have worked on each one's *Primary Sense of Being,* in which you establish a character's GENERAL *emotional makeup, attitude* and *actions*. When these traits are established, the next element to look at is the character's *Secondary Sense of Being,* which refers to the character's physical and/or emotional condition at a particular moment in time, i.e., the current scene. At this point, the director establishes the character's logical behavior/attitude relating to:

• Place (Environment);
• Time of Day;

- Accoutrements (Clothing);
- Momentary Emotional Condition;
- Momentary Physical Condition;
- Prior Place;
- Future Place;
- Props.

PLACE

A scene's environment is crucial to a character's actions and responses, meaning, his goals and actions. Read the following dialogue between two young men, DONALD and VINCENT:

> DONALD
> I shouldn't be here. Why am I in this dammed place? What am I doing here? All my life, Dad has controlled me.

> VINCENT
> Forget about it. Most parents are that way.

> DONALD
> Crap! I have no idea why he pushed me into this. I didn't want it. No way. I don't need to make—what Dad calls—a "name for myself."

> VINCENT
> Your father did what he thought best.

> DONALD
> His damned best, yes, so what am I to do now? Nothing. Listen to me. Nothing...nothing...

If this scene takes place in a college cafeteria, the environment, which would be exceedingly noisy, would have no impact on the scene.

Donald's Goal: To let off steam.

Vincent's Goal: To calm Donald down.

The environment of the scene now changes to a mountain shack; the dialogue remains the same. However, an addition has been made to the scene: Donald's father has convinced the two friends to take a mentally unstable cousin on a hike. During the hike, the man tries to kill them. It is night. Donald and Vincent, having escaped the killer, are hiding in the shack. They whisper. Now Donald's and Vincent's goals have changed:

Donald's Goal I: To accuse his father.

Donald's Goal II: To place the blame on his father for whatever might happen.

Vincent's Goal I: To close his ears to Donald's immature complaints.

Vincent's Goal II: To listen for sounds of the killer.

While Donald's frenzy builds, Vincent doesn't hear him. He is more concerned about Donald's psychotic cousin finding them, so he offers Donald only mechanical replies.

Now, let's change the environment to a foreign prison and the scenario to this: Donald and Vincent, both missionaries, have been jailed on the suspicion of espionage. They have just witnessed two of their cellmates being hauled away for execution. Donald and Vincent are catatonic with fear. Now, look at how Vincent's goals have changed:

Donald's Goal: To spit words out as to convince himself he is still alive. Alive? Alive for how long?"

Vincent's Goal II: He cannot emotionally or physically comfort Donald; all he wants to do is pray they survive.

TIME OF DAY

The time of day matters to most people. For example, in the morning, those who are early risers have energy, concentration and move with ease while those who are not, may be grouchy, slow to move and think, feel disconnected or are easily angered.

ACCOUTREMENTS (CLOTHING)

Clothing is an important element in character makeup because it can affect a character's movements (i.e., he may feel proud wearing one kind of clothing or uncomfortable and self-conscious in another). Being unsuitably dressed for the weather or a special occasion can also affect the character's mood.

MOMENTARY EMOTIONAL CONDITION

Any easy-going person, one with a positive attitude and a rosy outlook on life, can be aroused to great anger. Conversely, any grumpy and pessimistic character could find a brief moment in his day when he might loosen up a bit.

MOMENTARY PHYSICAL CONDITION

We come to know characters through their physicalness: sickness or health; exhaustion or well-being; hunger and thirst for satiation; age or youthfulness; affluence or poverty. These elements create the physical base of a character. Depending on physical conditions, a character will act / react differently to events.

PRIOR PLACE

Conditions existing in the scene immediately prior can greatly influence a character's behavior and attitude.

Examples

Scenario I — Prior Place: Eric is stuck on the freeway.

Scenario I — Current Place: Greeting his girlfriend, Eric is less loving than usual.

Scenario II — Prior Place: Claire has a wonderful day of shopping: she finds great bargains, has lunch with friends, hears exciting gossip.

Scenario II — Current Place: Coming home, Claire is assaulted by a messy house, unmade beds, unwashed dishes and a huge stack of bills. Her good mood enables her to take these disturbances in stride.

FUTURE PLACE

Events expected to happen following the current scene can definitely color a character's mood and consequent behavior.

Examples

Scenario I — Future Place: Sara exuberantly packs her bags because tomorrow, she and Bill are going on their long-planned cruise to the Greek Islands. Her movements are quick and efficient. Happily, she hums to herself.

Scenario II — Future Place: Arthur packs his bags for the annual obligatory fishing trip with his old, grumpy uncle. Arthur hates camping; the smell of fish makes him sick; he gets nervous sitting in a small boat for hours; he feels sorry for the worms he kills and silently apologizes to the poor creatures. And, worse, he must spend tortured hours listening to his uncle's stories about "the olden times when this here guy was a wee little shaver." Therefore, Arthur's face is dark and unfriendly as he carelessly throws clothes, insect repellent, aspirin and sunscreen into his backpack.

Looking at the examples given above, you can see that the mood of any scene is not necessarily determined by the content of the dialogue as by the situation and the environment.

<u>Exercise</u>

Select a short scene from a stage play. Without altering dialogue:
- Create a different situation;
- Create a different environment.

PART 3

CREATING
THE ON-SCREEN
IMAGE

Introduction

The director must develop the characters' *on-screen presence* rather than simply photographing the image of an actor speaking lines. In fact, when the director begins developing the characters, he must consider much more than dialogue; he must utilize camera angles and movement and lighting design as well as dialogue. To succeed at this effort, the director must put the viewer into the action. And, in order to do this, he should place himself into the viewer's shoes, deciding whether the viewer should be in the *omnipotent* or *subjective* position. Affecting the viewer's position is done through cinematography.

Each camera angle's visual effect contributes to or detracts from the film's narrative line and overall mood. Orchestrating camera setups and choreographing actor movements into visual-emotional unity is what good filmmaking is all about. Therefore, never look at a camera shot for its singular effect, but rather, consider each shot as part of a unit which will be edited into a sequence of film.

Part 3, therefore, discusses camera movement, viewpoint and editing used to create cinematic unity. These movements are a combination of the following elements:

- Movement;
- Viewpoint;
- Framing (Picturalization);
- Editing.

3.1 Movement

When preparing to direct a moving shot, don't bring the camera to the action; let the camera *participate* in the action. To do this, you must use one of three types of *Moving Shot*:
- *Primary Movement,* or, movement in front of the camera;
- *Secondary Movement,* or, movement of the camera itself;
- *Tertiary Movement,* or, movement created by a succession of shots captured by more than one camera used at the same time.

PRIMARY MOVEMENT

A movement (by an actor or an object) TOWARD or AWAY from the camera is more memorable than a LATERAL movement. You achieve more emphasis by having an actor walk to the camera or away from it, rather than by having him walk from the right side of the frame to the left; this is especially true for entrances and exits. But you must decide whether or not the scene requires such a strong dramatic expression.

If you decide on lateral movement, make certain your camera leads the movement (i.e., it should not trail the actor or the object). You must project ahead whether the movement continues in the same or opposite direction.

Example

A police car chases a bank robber's van. You'll likely take different shots of the police and robber cars (interior and exterior). However, pursuer and pursued MUST move in the SAME direction, as seen below:

```
EXT. ROAD

ON police car. [Left to right]

EXT. ROAD

ON van. [Left to right]

INT. VAN

The MAN drives, the WOMAN, gun in hand,
looks back over her shoulder at the ap-
proaching police car.

EXT. ROAD

Police car speeding up. [Left to right]
```

When cutting between subjects about to make contact, filming them from OPPOSITE directions is mandatory:

Example

```
EXT. ROAD

ON police car [Left side of frame]

EXT. ROAD

ON van. [Right side of frame]

INT. VAN

MEDIUM SHOT of MAN slamming on brakes.
[Right side of frame]

CU of boot on brake. [Neutral shot]

MEDIUM SHOT of WOMAN screaming. [Right side
of frame]

INT. POLICE CAR

MEDIUM SHOT. OFFICER slams on the brakes,
his body falls forward, the other officer
throws his body back. [Left side of frame]
```

If the pursuit changes into a scene of contact, simply have one of the parties (in this case, the police) sidetrack and—unexpectedly—approach the opponent from the opposite side.

SECONDARY MOVEMENT

Although utilizing camera movement creates provocativeness and excitement, use secondary movement with restraint. Most moving shots present lighting problems; all moving shots are time-consuming. Actors involved in scenes with camera movement must rehearse many times. Reminding the viewer of the camera's presence by over utilizing camera movement breaks the spell of the viewer's identification with the events on the screen. Most significantly, secondary movement presents a visual impression the viewer rarely experiences in real life. You CAN make a long dialogue scene come alive by using a combination of both primary and secondary movements, but stay away from boring two-shots and reversals (also known as "talking head" scenes). Applied with discretion and directed so that important issues are emphasized while those of lesser importance are de-emphasized, secondary movement can add positive impact to you film.

Secondary camera movements include:

- The Pan Shot;
- The Tilt Shot;
- The Dolly Shot;
- The Zoom Shot.

THE PAN SHOT

A *Pan Shot* emphasizes an object, person or situation by following up a primary movement. A Pan also might be used to adjust a shot.

Example

Pan Shot

INT. ROOM

ON MONK reading a book. He puts it down,
walks to the bookcase [*primary movement*]
places the book on a shelf. Pan with Monk
[*secondary movement*] as he walks to the
door.

Pan Shots are categorized as a *Survey Pan*; a *Tracking Pan*; and a *Whip Pan*. In a *Survey Pan*, the camera scans an area without a specific point of interest, such as panning a row of stationary objects. (If you opt for a Survey Pan, be sure the objects are fairly close together, or you'll end up with dead space on the screen.) If the viewer must be drawn to a specific moving object (i.e., a car, a rider, a group of hikers) the shot becomes a *Tracking Pan*, which bisects the subject's movement.

Example

Survey/Tracking Pans

EXT. FIELD

SURVEY Pan. HOLD on a group of Union soldiers on horseback. One of the soldiers
separates from the others. TRACK [*tracking
Pan*] with him as he rides away.

Concentrate on the tracked subject's speed and the line along which he moves. Notice that a Tracking Pan follows a lateral movement without changing the angle or distance of the moving object. The speed of a Pan Shot is determined by situation or storyline, or by the emotion the director wishes to arouse. An exceedingly slow Pan develops the viewer's anticipation, while a *Whip Pan*, which blurs all images, has a strong emotional impact if the viewer has been placed in the subjective position (into the hero's shoes).

THE TILT SHOT

In a *Tilt Shot,* the camera moves up or down. Because of its visual power, the Tilt is highly effective for creating suspense and is also effective in violent action scenes or in any other type of highly emotional scene with which the director wants the viewer to identify. For example, depending on the script's narrative, a *Down Tilt* on one character and an *Up Tilt* on another can be effective. But, use the Tilt Shot only if you intend to make a specific statement because, like other camera movements, the Tilt draws attention away from the drama and over to the director's techniques. (You want your audience to rave about your film, not your stylish camera movements!)

Example

Tilt Shot

```
EXT. BACKYARD

TILT DOWN slowly. Take in the lawn as the
grass softly moves in the breeze. TILT DOWN
more slowly—and more slowly. Now, ZOOM IN
on a rattlesnake ready to strike.
```

THE DOLLY SHOT

A *Dolly Shot* moves up to or away from a subject. When you *Dolly In,* the camera moves from a general shot to a specific detail as it gradually enlarges that detail. For example, if the camera shoots a store window display so the viewer sees everything in the window, and then Dollies In to a sculpture on a table in the display, that one *objet d'art* is thereby emphasized. A *Dolly Out* is opposite from the Dolly In: the camera moves from a subject in detail to a general shot. For example, you have a Medium Shot of a girl; when the camera Dollies Out, we see the girl in the middle of a huge party.

You will make a strong point by using a quick Dolly Shot; a slow Dolly Shot is better when making a subtle point. In any case, don't confuse the "Dolly In" shot with a Zoom Shot.

THE ZOOM SHOT

The *Zoom Shot* is a very rapid movement to or away from a subject. But be careful with the Zoom: this particular camera movement has been overused by many low-budget horror and/or action films and has therefore lost its effectiveness.

TERTIARY MOVEMENT

Tertiary Movement applies to a shot taken by two or more cameras at the same time: each camera captures the action from a different viewpoint. The Tertiary Movement is expensive and can create editing problems because of the many different angles involved. However, if you must film a major action scene, i.e., a car exploding, sinking into a lake, or rolling down a hill, you have no choice but to use Tertiary Movement in order to film the stunt in one take. After all, once the car has exploded or sunk or crashed, it will take time, money, energy and preparation to film the shot again.

UTILIZING CAMERA MOVEMENTS AND CAMERA LENSES

Throwing either the background or the foreground out of focus can help the director can make a dramatic statement. This movement, then, takes the viewer's attention from one part of the frame to another.

<u>Example</u>

```
INT. ROOM

MEDIUM SHOT on ABBY, left side of frame.
BOBBY [out of focus] appears in the right
side of frame. As Abby turns to look at
Bobby, rack focus on Bobby. [Now, Abby is
out of focus.
```

CAMERA LENSES

Your cinematographer will know the variety of lenses used in films, but you should be familiar with them, too. (Utilizing the correct lens in consort with physical action is one of the reasons why directors should have on-camera rehearsals.)

- *Standard Lens*. This is the 20mm lens, which captures the same angle as the human eyes.
- *Wide Angle Lens*, which is a lens of less than 25mm focal length (short focus). The most commonly used wide angle lens is the 12.5mm. This lens is useful in small enclosed spaces such as a car interior) but it should not be used for Close Ups (it has a tendency to distort) or for Medium Shots (it can create too much space between two characters).
- *Telephoto Lens*. This ranges upward to 75mm in focal length and bring distant action closer to the camera by compressing the foreground-to-background ratio.

DEPTH OF FIELD

The Depth of Field of any lens is defined as "range of acceptable sharpness." Depth of Field depends on:

- The focal length of the lens;
- The aperture setting;
- The lens, the subject and the distance between the

two. Generally speaking, the smaller the aperture setting, the greater depth of field. Following are some common questions you should discuss with your cinematographer:

- How important is the detail in the shot?
- How do you isolate a subject or object in the frame?
- Should the foreground and background relate during an action shot?

3.2 Viewpoint

The director's *viewpoint* (*the way of setting camera angles*) determines that shot's feeling of excitement or conventionality. Always keep in mind a shot's relation to the full sequence of shots; as usual, it must serve the plotline as well as develop the planned visual-emotional impact. Therefore, design shots with a specific reason in mind and not merely to promote your own sense of creativity or provocativeness. Viewpoint, broken down into the following categories, can be an important dramatic tool:

- Normal Viewpoint;
- High Angle Viewpoint;
- Low Angle Viewpoint;
- Canting Viewpoint;
- Close Up (CU) Viewpoint (combined with various angles).

THE NORMAL VIEWPOINT

If you place the camera at eye level with the character on screen (*Normal Viewpoint*), you put the viewer into the subjective position, thus emphasizing the viewer's identification with the character.

HIGH ANGLE

The camera placed higher than the character's eyeline is defined as a *High Angle Viewpoint*. Used with a wide angle lens, the High Angle shot is perfect when establishing such scenes as a landscape, a hockey game, or a dance in a huge ballroom. The High Angle was often used to visually interpret the relationship between characters. (To get an idea of this shot's effectiveness, watch the silent film, *The Phantom*

Of The Opera; Rupert Julian, 1925.) Currently, the High Angle shot is used sparingly to establish a dramatic point.

LOW ANGLE

Opposite of the High Angle, the *Low Angle Viewpoint* places the camera lower than the eyeline. Similar to the High Angle shot, the Low Angle is used infrequently and usually in a relationship sequence. However, Low Angle shots are helpful if you wish to eliminate unwanted foreground.

The combination of extreme Low Angle and High Angle shots is an effective visual combination in such genre films as horror and fantasy—if the combination is utilized in the appropriate narrative context. On the other hand, diminutive High and Low Angle, up-and-down shots (i.e., slightly above and slightly below the eyeline) are helpful because these camera positions make the viewer subconsciously aware of the characters' relationship to each other (when dialogue is not indicative).

CANTING

Canting the camera creates a *diagonal image* on screen. It is a powerful image, but again, it is one that should be used sparingly.

CLOSE UP

The *Close Up* can be the most powerful screen image for a director to use—if it is utilized correctly and within the context of the sequence being shot. Some directors go overboard with the Close Up, giving the viewer an array of "talking heads" scenes, thereby over utilizing the shot. When this happens, the Close Up's effectiveness diminishes.

Never cut from a Long Shot to a Close Up; rather, make the transition via a Medium Shot or a Dolly shot. Tracking the camera into a Close Up gives the actor a powerful position in relation to the camera; the same holds true for the actor directly facing the camera, if you frame him slightly to the right or left of the lens. For shots of longer duration or to give the on-screen image a more natural appearance, utilize a half-shoulder shot instead of a Close Up.

The *Extreme* (or, *Critical*) *Close Up* is often used in television series and movies, but it should be avoided on the motion picture screen. Unless the director wants to create the illusion of tremendous strength, the Extreme Close Up is usually overpowering and calls attention away from the on-screen events. (When using this shot, do not cut off the actor's chin.)

Always be fully aware that lighting is of the utmost importance in any Close Up shot.

3.3 Framing

Framing refers to the on-screen, three-dimensional effect of individual set-ups. Lighting contributes tremendously to this illusionary third dimension, but placement of subject and object is equally important to creating appropriate framing, which must contain:

- Balance;
- Symmetry.

BALANCE

Always arrange framing on the screen in such a way that one area does not outweigh the other. For example, action should not take place in one area of the frame while the other area is devoid of movement.

SYMMETRY

The subject in the frame should never be placed directly in the middle of the screen. The only exception to this is using the Extreme (or, Critical) Close Up. When using the Close Up, in order to effect symmetry and to create illusionary space on screen, have the actor face slightly to the right or left. If the actor looks to the right, position him somewhat to the left on the screen, and vice versa. If action takes place behind the actor, position the actor slightly to the side, utilizing a *Medium*, or *Three-Quarter Shot*. When filming a *Two-Shot*, do not shoot a scene in which the two actors are facing each other, nose to nose. A person's mouth and eyes transmit emotion; the static, bony parts of the chin and nose don't. In a Two-Shot, frame the actors side-by-side, having each one turn his head at a 45° angle as they face each other.

Gettysburg (Turner Pictures, 1993, Ronald F. Maxwell, 254 mins.) contains excellent examples of camera framing.

3.4 Editing

D. W. Griffith, an American film pioneer and the industry's first major producer-director (*The Filmgoer's Companion* by Leslie Halliwell. New York: New York, 1965) said, "The foundation of film art is editing." Griffith's statement is as valid today as it was during his filmmaking days, circa 1912.

In the editing process, a film's viewpoint and meaning can be heightened, diminished or changed by rearranging film shots, thus influencing the movie's rhythm, mood and visuals. The best editing should not be noticeable; it is difficult and senseless to give every frame of film significance. However, it is important that director and editor decide upon the smooth and logical editing of sequences. In good film editing, the editor shows the viewer what is happening on screen, lets the viewer participate in situations and events, but never calls attention to the editing techniques.

A completed film consists of two separate elements:
- individual shots;
- a sequence of edited shots compiled from the individual shots.

Directors and editors may emphasize individual shots or they may rely on a combination of seemingly insignificant shots or they may highlight shots of longer duration pulled together by Secondary Movement. Regardless which technique you select for any particular scene (or sequence), view each shot (or sequence) as part of your film's overall continuity. It is the amplification of the film's basic narrative that enables the viewer to relate the sequence on screen to events, dialogue or situations previously viewed.

Perhaps you have done some editing yourself; hopefully, the editor on your film is skilled and experienced. Nevertheless, some basic editing conventions are listed below.

- Show the viewer what he needs to see in order to ask himself, *What Will Happen Next? (Motive).* Then, cut to the *Response.*
- *Always Cut On Movement.* For example, the camera shows Elisa as she *raises* her glass. Cut to Doug as he *shakes* his head. [*DO NOT cut to Doug first, sitting motionless, then shaking his head.*)
- *Never cut from a Pan Shot to a Stationary Shot.*

<u>Examples</u>

Motive

EXT. MOUNTAIN

WE SEE a group of hikers. Suddenly, one recoils [**Motive**].

CUT TO

Big Foot approaching [**Response**].

Cut On Movement

INT. CAR—DAY

CU of foot SLAMMING on the car brake.

CUT TO

MEDIUM SHOT. Bert's body falls against the windshield. [*Cut during Bert's fall, not after Bert has hit the windshield.*]

EXT. ROAD—DAY

Bert's car crashes against a wall.

Pan Shot to a Stationary Shot

Don't:

```
EXT. STREET

Three-quarter Pan SHOT. Mark walking up to
George.

CUT TO

George (MEDIUM SHOT) as Mark walks into
frame.
```

Do:

```
EXT. STREET

Pan with Mark as he walks up to George.
DOLLY IN when MARK stands next to GEORGE.
```

Many movement shots should be worked out in your shooting script, before principal photography begins. Even the best editing could not eradicate the shooting mistakes listed below. Only advanced preparation would have helped.

- *Never cut from a Long Shot to a half-shoulder (Close Up); rather, have the camera Dolly In.*
- *Eyelines.* The actor establishes an *Eyeline* by looking at another actor or at an object. Trying to edit to-gether shots that contain wrongly-placed eyelines makes an editor climb the proverbial "wall." It is the director's job to coordinate an actor's eyeline with the targeted object, even though the object may not be filmed until days later.

Examples

Long Shot to a Half-Shoulder

Don't:

```
INT. STORE

LONG SHOT of Susan walking up to the
store's counter.
```

```
CUT TO
```

MEDIUM SHOT of Susan standing in front of the counter. She reaches into her bag and pulls out a gun.

Do:

```
INT. STORE
```

LONG SHOT of Susan entering store. DOLLY IN to a three-quarter shot as she walks up to the counter. DOLLY IN to MEDIUM SHOT as Susan stands in front of the counter. She reaches into her purse.

```
CUT TO
```

CLOSE UP of her hand pulling out a gun.

Eyelines

Don't:

```
EXT. PLAINS
```

MEDIUM SHOT of MAN looking down. We SEE an eagle circling overhead.

Do:

```
EXT. PLAINS
```

MEDIUM SHOT of MAN looking up. We SEE an eagle circling overhead.

Don't hesitate to direct your actors' eyelines in group scenes, especially if some actors are seated but others are standing. Because editing group scenes is tricky, it's best to give your editor as much to work with as possible. Therefore, shoot a *Master Shot* of the entire group. (Having a Master Shot saves nerves and editing time.) Then, shoot Close Ups or Medium Shots of smaller pairings. If you're going to shoot a Master Shot simply for the editor's guidance, why not tape it on video; 35mm raw stock can be expensive.

- *Don't cut on lateral action from opposite sides.* If you do, the directions will be reversed on screen.
- *When cutting dialogue scenes, do not regularly cut at the end of each phrase.* Rather, (1) cut from Actor A in the middle of a phrase to (2) a Voice Over (VO), then to (3) Actor B listening. (This type of cut works especially well in camera reversals.) Later, to avoid predictability, (1) cut Actor A at the end of his lines (preferably short ones) and to (2) Actor B's verbal response.
- *Shoot Complementary Angles in Reverse.* Only complementary angles can be edited smoothly. If the actor looks to his RIGHT (in front of the camera) he will be looking to his LEFT on the screen (i.e., Actor A looks at Actor B who is positioned to A's RIGHT, off-camera, in reverse). On screen, Actor A looks to his LEFT. This way, Actors A and B make eye contact.)
- *Maintain Directional Continuity.* If a character moves in one direction in one shot, the following shot must show the character continuing in the same direction. Since this is not always possible, the wise director bridges two directional scenes with a *Neutral Shot.* This principle is especially important if one shot starts in location A and continues in location B.

Example

EXT. STREET—NIGHT

Anne runs along a deserted street. LONG SHOT (lateral movement to the left) as she turns a corner.

CUT TO

Three-quarter Shot, front view. Anne stops to catch her breath [*Neutral Shot*].

```
CUT TO

MEDIUM SHOT of Anne running (lateral move-
ment to the right).
```

- *Cut In, Cut Out.* Most Long Shots do not hold the viewer's attention. Therefore, keep the duration of a Long Shot short and CUT IN to three-quarter shots. When editing, do not have characters change their positions from the previously established ones. Do not break continuity between the Cut In and what has happened in the Long Shot, but, rather, move the camera closer, i.e., Long Shot to three-quarter Shot; three-quarter Shot to Medium Shot. Cutting Out indicates the camera is moving to a wider shot. The progression of shots listed above would still apply, i.e., Medium Shot to three-quarter Shot; three-quarter Shot to Long Shot.
- *Jump Cut.* This occurs when the middle portion of a shot is cut out, or, the viewer watches only the beginning and end of a shot. As a result, the Jump Cut calls attention to itself. Jump Cuts are mostly used for comedic value.
- *Parallel cutting* (or, *Intercutting*). In Parallel editing, the action cuts away and then cuts back again.

Example

```
INT. TRAIN

Two-Shot of couple: He reads a newspaper,
she looks out the window.

EXT. TRAIN

Zooming along.

INT. TRAIN

Now, he snores. She steals the billfold
from his coat pocket.
```

- *Change of speed*. The mood of a scene can be enhanced by varying its tempo as you cut from shot to shot. Excitement builds by quickening the pace (i.e., shots of shorter duration) while exhaustion shows by slowing the pace. In a scene of two lovers, the pace of the editing will be more leisurely if they are walking along a lake shore than if they are running to catch a plane.
- *Always establish the environment and the characters' positions within this environment.*

Exercise

Utilizing the editing points reviewed above, write a shooting script for the following scenario. Tape it and then edit it.

```
Louise returns from work. The phone rings.
She listens to the incoming message. She
almost picks up the receiver, but decides
against it. She starts supper by going to
the refrigerator, taking out a few items,
placing them on the counter. She stops
suddenly, rushes back to the phone and
starts dialing. She hangs up. On her way
back to the kitchen, the phone rings again.
Louise, frozen, leans against the counter.
```

3.5 Editing Concepts

The team of director and editor works within the framework of two editing concepts:

- Continuity Editing (point-of-view editing, invisible editing);
- Dynamic Editing (subjective editing, emphatic editing).

Depending on plotline and on the emotional-visual impact desired, both concepts will overlap once the film completes production and arrives on the editing bench.

CONTINUITY EDITING

If you wish to stress the FACTS in a scene the editor will utilize *Point of View* editing. If the scene is based primarily on MOVEMENT (Primary or Secondary Movement), then *Invisible* editing is appropriate. Both editing techniques put the viewer in the *omnipotent position*.

Example

Point of View Editing

```
EXT. VICTORIAN MANSION—NIGHT

Vicky's car stops in front of the mansion.

INT. VICKY'S CAR—NIGHT

Vicky fumbles through her purse and pulls
out a gun. She looks up.

VICKY'S POV

The mansion.

BACK TO SCENE

Vicky gets out of the car.
```

EXT. VICTORIAN MANSION—NIGHT

Vicky, carefully so as not to make a sound, closes the car door. Pan WITH Vicky as she walks up to the mansion and slowly opens the front door.

INT. VICTORIAN MANSION—NIGHT

ON Vicky entering.

VICKY'S POV

The shadowy hallway.

BACK TO SCENE

Vicky points her gun.

Invisible editing depends heavily on Primary and Secondary movement and on Parallel cutting. In Invisible Editing, movement becomes the "star" of the scene.

Example

Invisible Editing

EXT. STREET—NIGHT

ON Vicky's car, driving down the street. [*Neutral front shot*.] The car moves closer and closer to the camera until its headlights fill the screen.

INT. VICKY'S CAR—NIGHT

MEDIUM SHOT ON Vicky as she fumbles through her purse, reaching for something.

CLOSE UP

Vicky's gun.

BACK TO SCENE

Vicky driving.

EXT. STREET—NIGHT

ON Vicky's car, driving up to the curb. The car stops. Vicky gets out of the car. She pauses, looks up.

VICKY'S POV

A Victorian mansion looms against the moon-filled sky.

Pan WITH Vicky walking up to the front door.

INT. VICTORIAN MANSION—HALLWAY—NIGHT

A shadowy hallway. A door opens a crack.

EXT. VICTORIAN MANSION—NIGHT

ON Vicky, opening the front door.

INT. VICTORIAN MANSION—HALLWAY—NIGHT

The door opens wider. A dark FIGURE emerges, hides in a corner.

EXT. VICTORIAN MANSION—NIGHT.

Vicky slips into the house.

INT. VICTORIAN MANSION—HALLWAY—NIGHT

Softly, Vicky closes the door, leans against it, looks up and points her gun.

DYNAMIC EDITING

Contrary to Continuity Editing, which aims to convey meaning, *Dynamic Editing* uses *visualization to create dramatic action, as well as to increase tension and emotion.* Dynamic editing tries to strengthen a scene's impact by providing more intensity to the on-screen situation. Dynamic editing puts the viewer into the *subjective position* or, the "hero's shoes," by utilizing the techniques of *Subjective* Editing or *Emphatic* Editing.

Subjective Editing works best for suspense sequences and in setting the motive for the viewer's question, "What will happen next?"

Example

Subjective Editing

EXT. VICTORIAN MANSION—NIGHT

Vicky's car stops in front of the mansion.

INT. VICKY'S CAR—NIGHT

Vicky looks up.

VICKY'S POV

The mansion looms darkly in the moonlit sky.

INT. VICKY'S CAR—NIGHT

Vicky takes a deep breath. PULL IN as she brushes her fingertips over her mouth. Again, she looks up.

VICKY'S POV

TILT camera. The mansion, now looming darker and closer, seems to tumble on top of her.

INT. VICKY'S CAR—NIGHT

Quickly, Vicky reaches for her purse, pulls out a gun.

CLOSE UP

Vicky's gun.

BACK TO VICKY

as she hastily gets out of the car.

EXT. VICTORIAN MANSION—NIGHT

PULL IN, TRACK WITH Vicky as she hurries to the mansion's front door. She hesitates for a moment. Then, she slowly opens the door.

INT. VICTORIAN MANSION—HALLWAY—NIGHT

ON Vicky

as she softly closes the door. She leans against it. Listens. Points her gun. Everything is quiet.

```
VICKY'S POV

The hallway's shadowy details.

ESTABLISHING Pan

The corner is steeped in darkness. There is
an old-fashioned umbrella stand, wallpaper
hanging down in shreds. Then, an unexpected
ZOOM to a dark figure huddled on the stair-
case.
```

Emphatic Editing relies on *contrast*; rhythm and visual patterns are juxtaposed against each other. Emphatic Editing often depends upon on parallel cutting to express an emotion or to make a point.

Example

Emphatic Editing

(Exterior scenes remain the same as in Subjective Editing, but interior scenes switch to the Emphatic Editing technique.)

```
INT. VICTORIAN MANSION—NIGHT

Vicky enters. Slowly, ever so slowly, she
closes the door.

VICKY'S POV

The dark staircase.

FLASHCUT TO

a BRIDE dressed in a turn-of-the-century
wedding gown; she stands on the stairs.

BACK TO VICKY

standing motionless.

VICKY'S POV

The dark staircase.

BACK TO VICKY

pointing her gun. She hesitantly moves a
few steps into the hallway. She looks up.
```

```
VICKY'S POV

The dark staircase looming in front of her.

BACK TO VICKY

as she takes another few steps, keeping her
eyes on the staircase.

VICKY'S POV

another FLASHCUT on the bride.

BACK TO VICKY

straightening her back she advances into
the hall. SWISH Pan to dark figure leaning
against the wall.
```

In all of the above interpretations of the main action—*Vicky enters the Victorian mansion*—the action reverts to the script's seemingly uncomplicated situation:

```
EXT. VICTORIAN MANSION—NIGHT

Vicky's car stops in front of the mansion.
She gets out of the car. Pan with her as
she walks up to the mansion and enters.

INT. VICTORIAN MANSION—HALLWAY—NIGHT

Vicky enters. She closes the door, listens
and points her gun. Suddenly the mansion's
eerie, other worldly atmosphere reaches out
to her.
```

It is this *other worldly atmosphere* the director makes evident to the viewer by his creation of the shooting script and via his (and the editor's) projected editing process.

By looking at these various editing patterns, it is obvious the director cannot wait until the editing process begins before giving his picture a certain tone or ambiance. Each film's mood, the scenes' continuity with each other, the foreshadowing of future events, must be established prior to principal photography. In other words, the director must decide upon many details of the editing concept while preparing his shooting script. Needless to say, one cannot completely rely on the shooting script because there may be location changes, budgetary considerations or technical delays. Any kind of difficulty may force the director to adjust his filmic "blueprint."

Exercises

Utilizing one the given editing concepts:
- Write a shooting script for *Vicky And The Victorian Mansion*. Tape and edit it.
- Write a shooting script of your own. Tape and edit it.
- While studying one of your favorite films, pay attention to its editing concepts.

PART 4

THE
ELEMENTS
OF SOUND
AND LIGHT

4.1 Sound, Dialogue And Music

SOUND

In addition to the images on the screen, *sound* can give the audience information necessary for understanding the plot. Ambient sound, music and sound effects—all of which should express emotion and mood—can *influence the viewer's response* to the visual image. For example, the sound of a dripping faucet can draw attention to a character's anxiety; the sound of a crying child as a judge slams his gavel can answer the viewer's question about which parent is awarded custody of him; the sounds of laughter and music tell the audience that a couple toasting each other are reveling in happiness. If used appropriately, sound can dramatize a situation AND give rise to ideas.

Picture and sound should work in tandem to create the mood or emotion of a scene, though, at times, sound can be a dominating force. Be careful about overusing music and sound effects; if overly used, these two elements can easily act against the viewer's identification with the situation on the screen.

There are many different sound techniques used in films today, including:

- *Ambient Sound.* These are *natural sounds*, i.e., waves slamming against a sea wall; street traffic; birds in trees. So, whenever possible, record the available ambient sounds while you are at a specific location.

Example

```
INT. FACTORY—DAY

The FOREMAN has achieved his promotion by
cheating. Shoulders hunched, he sits at his
desk while WE HEAR machinery WHIRRING and
HOWLING, sounding quite threatening.
```

- *Voice Distortion.* This is an increase or decrease in the voice volume of a character which parallels the listening character's perception of him.
- *Separate Sound.* This type of sound can be used to create a counterpoint against the visual image on screen.

Example

```
INT. HOSPITAL ROOM—NIGHT

A terminally ill WOMAN smiles as she remem-
bers the joyful laughter of her children
playing.
```

- *Overlapping Sound.* In this sound technique, one sound takes precedence over another.

Example

```
INT. HOSPITAL ROOM—NIGHT

A terminally ill WOMAN smiles as she remem-
bers the joyful laughter of her children
playing.

After awhile, the sound of ringing CHURCH
BELLS overlaps the children's laughter. The
bells grow louder until WE HEAR—shattering—
a HAMMER STRIKE METAL. For a moment [sound
and picture working in tandem] a bright
light fills the screen). This is followed
by SILENCE as the woman's image fades from
the screen.
```

- *Disjunctive Sound*. This is a technique in which sound does not precisely refer to the situation on screen, or to the character's emotion, yet it explains both in a subliminal way.

Example

```
EXT. CIVIL WAR LOCATIONS—MONTAGE

Farmer WILLIAM, who has no idea what the
Civil War is about, has dutifully left his
farm, young wife and infant child. The
SOUND OF DRUMBEATS—sometimes faintly, at
other times, unforgiving—is HEARD every so
often. The sound hangs over William in
bivouac, during respite in a tavern, and
becomes reality as he marches into battle.
```

An excellent example of creative sound integration can be found in *Mr. Holland's Opus* (Touchstone, 1995, Stephen Herek, 142 mins.).

Exercise

Write short scenes for the following scenarios, paying close attention to sound and visual integration.
- William says good-bye to his wife and child.
- An uncomfortable William has a drink in a tavern.
- Afraid of a looming battle, William sits in his bivouac, writing a letter to his wife.
- William marches into battle.

RECORDED DIALOGUE

When recording dialogue during film production, never skimp on equipment; you should insist on only the very best. Many professionals consider Nagra as the manufacturer of the top-of-the-line equipment, if operated by a skilled sound engineer. You still should pay close attention to the *boom operator*. On a multimillion production, an *assistant sound engineer* usually operates the boom microphone. On a low-budget film, this position is most likely to be handled by a production assistant (unless the sound engineer's crew includes one or two boom handlers). Before entrusting a PA with this all-important job, consider the following caveats:

- *Watch for boom shadows,* which can make any shot unusable.
- When blocking the actors in three-quarter shots and two-shots, *make sure the boom operator moves* with them. Rehearse the shot. Ask actors to avoid any unplanned (and therefore unrehearsed) movements.
- *Have the boom microphone positioned in front of the actor,* opposed to directly over his head.
- *The boom microphone cannot follow vertical movement,* therefore block your scenes in lateral movements. Also, advise your actors not to lean down while speaking. (This applies mostly to Medium Shots.)
- *If you must cover two actors with a single boom microphone, place it between the actors.* Also, to avoid constant volume adjustment for the sound engineer, have each actor slightly move his head in a lateral position while speaking dialogue.
- *Advise the sound engineer to watch the audio balance.* He always should favor the weaker voice.

SOUND EDITING

A sound laboratory (or a general post-production facility) will transfer your recorded sound tape to *magnetic film* (35mm). In addition, the sound lab will provide the filmmakers with a 1/4-inch tape; this is necessary for the creation of the (expensive) optical track, which will be processed by an optical laboratory.

During the editing process, the sound track literally must be handled with "kid gloves." Before proceeding to the final "mix" of the film (the process in which all the different sounds—dialogue, music, ambient sound, etc.— are mixed together) the sound editor must deal with the following processes:

- Sound Selection;
- Sound Sequencing;
- Sound Correction.

SOUND SELECTION

The process of deciding upon the music, ambient sounds and sound effects for specific points is called *Sound Selection*.

SOUND SEQUENCING

The sound editor and the director decide which sequences of sound segments will be used AND which type of transitions should be used between them, including:

- *The Segue,* in which one sound gradually but completely fades out while the next sound fades in.
- *The Crossfade,* in which one sound partially fades out while the next sound fades in.
- *The Straight Cut,* in which one sound goes straight to the next sound. (This is the preferred transition for dialogue sequences.)
- *Sound Loops.* Sometimes made from ambient sounds, a sound loop is a length of film (usually between four and five feet) that is spliced together and plays continuously; it can be edited into the film at any time.

Sometimes, ambient sounds recorded on location may prove unusable. Don't worry, an electronic device called a *graphic equalizer* can manipulate these sound inconsistencies. However, if your film is a tender love story set in the 18th Century and the sound of an airplane overhead interrupts the lovers' whispered confidences, you have no choice but to "dub in" (or "loop in") the dialogue between the actors at a later date. But, don't make dubbing a habit! Most, if not all, dubbed sequences give a film that "foreign" look in which all dialogue is badly dubbed into English.

SOUND MIXING

The *Mixing Session*—the time during post-production when your movie takes shape—is either an exhilarating or a frustrating experience, depending upon the amount of your preparation.

A number of sound tracks (each recorded on magnetic film) form the basis for the Mixing Session, including tracks for dialogue, music and sound effects. Make certain the dialogue track is removable from the other sound tracks because foreign buyers usually supply their own dialogue track. After the sound editor has completed his job, *start marks* are added. These marks are created by punching a small hole eight or nine frames ahead of the picture frame; a prerecorded beep tone is placed on the sound track's nonperforated edge. Sync marks are needed for proper synchronization when joining sound and picture, and when joining opticals and sound with picture.

Post-production facilities usually prefer *footage counters*. Therefore, have the sound editor supply the sound mixer with a cue sheet, with columns for each sound track and each picture track.

MUSIC

Music can *advance action* in a scene; it can *link dialogue*; it can *explain the on-screen environment*; it can *tell the viewer about a character's emotions*. But, music should never call attention to itself at the expense of the action or dialogue or event presented on-screen. In the same way that successful editing is not SEEN, music that is most effective should not be HEARD.

Music presents a strong contrast to the natural, ambient sounds surrounding us all day. But, since the era of silent "flickers," music has played an integral part in films. Therefore, never mislead the viewer by using music to create an emotion that is contrary to the event on screen.

Example

```
EXT. MIDDLE OF NOWHERE—MIDNIGHT

It's rainy, sleeting and cold. NINA (for
reasons we don't yet understand) walks up
to an abandoned farm house in the middle of
nowhere.
```

If filmed in the *omnipotent viewpoint*, the audience already will know the place is haunted. Therefore, don't ruin the viewer's dramatic involvement by adding music that underscores suspense. Music should show Nina's emotion and not emphasize the viewer's emotion. (Remember, Nina does not have the slightest idea what's waiting for her in the haunted farmhouse.) However, if Nina is aware of the impending danger, then it is acceptable for music to underscore her fear.

It is up to the producer to select the type of music he wants for the film, whether it be commissioning a composed score; utilizing prerecorded or, "canned" music (the least expensive and often the most effective source of music); or employing existing music.

Do not add to the producer's problems by insisting upon specific existing music. For instance, if a musical number is still under copyright, acquisition of it for your film may be time-consuming and expensive. Information regarding existing copyrights can be obtained from ASCAP (the American Society of Composers, Authors and Publishers) or from the U.S. Copyright Office (in Washington DC) However, neither agency can grant you the use of any copyrighted material. Synchronization rights must be negotiated through the music's publisher.

If you plan to use music in the public domain, i.e., a Sonata by Mozart, make sure that all rights do, in fact, belong in the public domain. In a situation where public domain music is used, the producer can have a new recording of the piece made, or, if an existing recording is to be used, the producer must pay a license fee to the music company (or studio) which owns the particular recording. All published music is subject to performance royalties.

4.2 Lighting

Lighting in film is both *expressive* and *functional*. Every image on screen needs lighting to convey its dramatic content to the viewer and to make that image as dynamic as possible. Good lighting can clarify environment, season, time of day and atmosphere. Think about it: every setting— i.e., forest, seashore, small town Main Street, cluttered kitchen—exudes a different atmosphere on a sunny day than when night falls and spreads its blanket of darkness.

Light is particularly important when combined with Color. The way light falls on colors plays a vital part in the creation of an emotional response to the image on screen. In addition, color often carries symbolic association for people; depending on the way a particular color is lit, it can change at any moment. Colors creatively coordinated within the limitations of a frame have the power to establish motive. For instance, let's imagine a scene showing Henry VIII and Anne Boleyn in a tower. If the background is lit with dark shadows and floating gray colors while a *zinger* sharply illuminates King Henry's face, then the King's motive in coming to the tower has been established. On the other hand, a sudden gust of sunshine striking through the background of the tower will give the viewer hope that Anne may survive.

Light is also important in the creation of *space*. Striking a balance between light and dark provides the illusion of a three-dimensional space.

LIGHTING THE SET

Lighting a film takes skill and intuition and a keen sense of the way shadow and light offset or complement each other.

Depending on the storyline, lighting may only need to "shed light," or, conversely, it can play an integral part of the visual-emotional design. Raindrops shimmering on leaves, a highlighted perfume bottle sitting on a cluttered dressing table, a table lamp creating an island of welcoming light in a dark room—all these small details can build mood or emphasize a character element.

As mentioned before (1.1, "All About Teamwork"), you and the cinematographer should discuss the lighting at length prior to commencing principal photography. Hopefully the two of you communicate well and support each other. The cinematographer should understand and respect your ideas for atmosphere, dramatic impact and theme. On the other hand, you must be supportive of the DP's visions while also realizing that some of his ideas simply cannot be managed due to budget and time constraints.

At times, "soft" lighting may be all a scene requires. Then again, especially when directing sequences with movement, you may need to change the lighting for every camera setup. This can be time-consuming and expensive and, at times (i.e., on location), impossible. In such cases, it may be best to decide upon workable overall lighting and move as few lights as necessary.

LIGHTING TECHNIQUES

Following is a brief overview of lighting techniques. Be cautioned that this overview will not teach you how to set up lights (that job belongs to the cinematographer and his gaffing crew), but will offer basic types of lighting that may be useful for creating certain kinds of images.

BASIC LIGHTING SETUP

These setups apply to interior and exterior shots and serve countless variations on the Long Shot, Medium Shot and Close Up.

- *Keylight.* These *directional lights* are the principal source of illumination. Usually, they are set up in front of or above a subject. Depending on the scene to be filmed, keylights may be hard or soft.

- *Backlight.* This technique *separates a character from his background*, giving form to hair and clothing (elements that, under different lighting circumstances, may blend into the background and get lost on the screen). If used in a Close Up, directly behind the actor, the light will soften his features. If the backlight is too strong, it will cast an undesirable *halo effect* around the actor. Usually, backlights are set up at a 45° angle from the background. Actors and objects should be placed at least six feet away from the background. If a bright background makes the actor's face look too shadowy, use a *fill light*. Be careful not to have too much contrast between lit and unlit areas; both should blend harmoniously. *Barn doors* (shutters attached to the light) will help adjust the light beams.

- *Fill lights* soften a scene and are extremely important to *balancing the keylight* that has been placed on the side. In Long Shots, fill lights are used to pick up background detail. Fill lights also serve to adjust shadowy areas. If the fill light appears too harsh, place a *scrim* (veil) over the light.

LIGHTING FOR INTERIORS

Lighting an interior will depend on the time of day you wish to create on screen. This usually presents few problems when shooting on a controlled soundstage, but may cause some minor worries when on location. First, eliminate all natural light by covering windows with black cloth before setting up the lights. Then, for daytime effects (whether you're filming on location or on a soundstage), always give the illusion of natural light shining through windows.

For night setups, create interplay between light and shadowy areas by using *directional lighting*—underlight the foreground but keylight all the characters. Using *rim lights* gives added intensity to facial expressions.

LIGHTING FOR EXTERIORS

Remember, light changes as the day progresses. An outdoor area at daybreak looks different at noon and more different still when dusk sets in. Therefore, when shooting an outdoor scene on location, be prepared to deal with rapidly changing light conditions. For example, a gazebo that was steeped in sunshine during filming of all Long Shots miraculously (no, fatally) turns gray as clouds appear. As your crew sets up for the Two-Shots, Reversals and Close Ups, it starts to rain. Your shooting day is over: the crew must pack up and money is wasted as everyone waits out the storm. (Location fees, equipment rentals, crew salaries and day player fees must be paid whether the crew works or not.) If you are directing a multimillion production, the producer most likely will take a one-day delay in stride. However, it is quite different if you are working on a low-budget film, when every day and every dollar counts.

Below are some practical suggestions to consider when lighting your sets. I have used the following practices many times:

- Make certain your production manager has arranged for a generator, in case of an electrical blackout.
- Shoot all Long Shots in as short a time as possible, to make certain light intensity does not change dramatically. If the lighting does sustain dramatic changes, editing these shots into a visually smooth sequence is almost impossible.
- Have your still photographer take slides of the locations. Then, if your shooting day is interrupted and you cannot return to a specific location to finish because of lighting alterations, don't worry. Go to a soundstage later, project these background slides and film the missing shots. If the stills are taken by an experienced photographer, there won't be ANY difference on screen between the actual location and the stage.

You need exterior lighting especially when filming Close Ups. Avoid direct sunlight or water reflections; these light sources can make the prettiest face look haggard.

If your shooting budget is unlimited, take your chances and shoot all the Long Shots first, then set up for the rest. As the crew sets up for Two-Shots and Reversals, try to approximate the previous lighting qualities by setting up a minor lighting plot consisting of keylights, backlights and fill lights.

SOFT LIGHTING PLOT

A *Soft Lighting Plot* (or, the *Basic Lighting Setup* mentioned earlier in this chapter) refers to *light distributed evenly over an area.* Many television shows and most television comedies use this type of plot. It's also useful when directing a low-budget film; or if you are pressed for time and money; or if a more detailed plot is not necessary for that particular scene. The Soft Light Plot permits actors to move freely (without setting up additional lights) in Three-quarter and Long Shots; it requires less lighting equipment and, therefore, less setup time.

SPECIFICS ABOUT LIGHTS

- A *Rim light* is a backlight that adds additional illumination to an actor or object.
- A *Zinger* is an extremely hard light that practically "hits" an actor or object. In horror films, zingers often are used in conjunction with Zoom Shots.
- A *Kicker* illuminates one side of the actor's face.
- *Soft Light* can be achieved by placing a scrim over the light fixture. This type of lighting should not be confused with the Soft Lighting Plot.
- *Baselight* refers to the minimum amount of lighting necessary for any camera to operate properly.
- *Incandescent Light* is the amount of light FALLING ON a scene.
- *Reflected Light* is the amount of light REFLECTED OFF a scene.
- *Additive Color.* Different colored gels placed over the lights will change, diminish or intensify that setting's color aspects. Mixing the basic colors—red, green and blue—will give you a variety of colors.
- *Unmotivated light sources*, i.e., keylights, backlights, fillers, are neutral and do not relate to environment or mood identification.
- *Motivated light sources*, i.e., desk lamp, streetlight, identify the environment. Avoid these light sources interfering with your overall lighting plot.

- *Background Light,* not to be confused with backlights, illuminates the background, not objects or characters, thereby giving the viewer the perception of time of day or the mood of the scene.
- *Hard Light/Soft Light. Hard light casts shadows* and is generated from a small, single light source. The *arc* is the hardest of this type of light currently in general use. In conjunction with the appropriate camera lens, the arc directs light into distinctive beams. *Soft light does not cast shadows* and is generated from various light sources. Lighting can fall between the two extremes.
- *Diffused Light* illuminates large areas with indistinct light beams. For example, *floodlights* are diffused light sources. Use *barn doors* to direct light beams and *flags* (metal attachments) to cast only a few shadows.
- *Low Key.* This effect is created by directing light to cut through the shadows of a dark background. Underlight some characters and highlight others. *The Silence Of The Lambs* (Orion, Jonathan Demme, 1991) shows good use of Low Key Lighting.
- *High Key.* Exactly opposite of Low Key Lighting, in High Key Lighting, most of the frame is well-lit and soft lights are used. Most musicals, such as *My Fair Lady* (Warner Bros., George Cukor, 1964) and *The Sound Of Music,* (20th Century-Fox, Robert Wise, 1965) depend on High Key Lighting.
- *Directional Lighting* illuminates a relatively small area with a small but distinctive light beam. For example, light seeping through the window of a dark room encircles a child sitting in a corner. *Spotlights* are directional light sources. In a Long Shot, directional lights are used to create depth of field and to offer a

separation of plane in order to give the scene a three-dimensional effect. Scrims and barn doors direct the light beams.

COLOR AND COLOR TEMPERATURE

Color temperature refers to *color consistency,* or the way colors keep their levels of intensity. Certain situations can make it difficult to maintain color consistency, including the following:

- *Filming on location.* As in the challenges of natural light changes, color consistency can be a difficult problem to confront because, subject to the location's light conditions, color temperature may also change constantly.
- *Raw stock.* When purchased from different manufacturers, raw stock does not always match and this can greatly affect the color consistency. For example, raw stock from Kodak has slightly different pigments than raw stock from Fuji. Trying to temper the changes by using jells over the lights won't necessarily unify the color values. Therefore, it is best to use only one kind of raw stock during the filming of your film.
- *Timing.* Supervise the computerized timing process of your film because during this procedure, your carefully selected hues may be watered down.

PART 5

THE
DIRECTOR
AND THE
ACTOR

Introduction

The material of the director's creativeness is the
creativeness of the actor.   — *Stanislavski*

By the time you are ready to begin working with your cast, probably you have arrived at a clear picture of the characters in your film. However, don't put yourself in a mental or emotional straitjacket. Keep an open mind throughout every aspect of working with the actors—during casting sessions, rehearsals and principal photography.

As the director, you will direct the script as written, but you also may interpret events and characters differently than the writer. The key actors will be guided by your interpretation of the script, but they also will decipher these guidelines in their own way. Actually, it is your responsibility to balance the various interpretations of the script (i.e., yours, the writer's, the actors', etc.). This is what honest directing is all about.

If your film features mind-boggling special effects or nerve-tingling action, still do everything in your power to expose its human side. Every film has the potential for presenting characters as living, breathing human beings; don't ignore this potential in your film. Although the actors may not be your film's central element, don't let them become marionettes to the action or special effects. Work with them and combine their creative input into your vision. On the other hand, don't become a "traffic cop," telling the actors where to stand, how to move and making such suggestions as, "Now, look happy," or "How about sighing as you hit your mark." If you do, the actors will walk all over you. Maintain control of the actors, but don't destroy their individuality because the careful channeling of their creative energy determines much of your film's effectiveness. Therefore, respect your actors' creative freedom, but help them clarify the LOGIC of their actions and reactions, which never should come from "left field."

If an actor's performance is controlled by his desire to enhance his own showing, the result will be a weakened film; he must follow his character's *line of action* established during your previous script analysis. Therefore, persuade your actors to search for emotions based upon their characters' goals and / or needs. Don't make them perform the role as you would have played the part; this temptation is overwhelming if you are also an actor yourself. As you work with actors, keep the following issues in mind:

- Discover each actor's creative capacity and expand on it. Do not let an ego-inspired performance slip past you. Editing cannot correct pretentious posing.
- Don't accept a skilled but shallow performance. However, this caveat DOES NOT apply to your film's only "bankable" star (or, the main reason why you're making the film in the first place). After assuring that you have surrounded your star with effective actors, you must diplomatically accept any performance he delivers.
- If you have serious difficulties with an actor, is the impasse your fault?
- Don't over theorize about the script's characters, thereby confusing your actors. While the characters' back stories may be important, they also may have little to do with the acting tasks at hand.
- Listen to and give your actors' suggestions serious consideration. But, be sure to ask yourself these questions:

1) How does the actor's interpretation relate to the overall storyline?
2) Is the actor's performance in accordance with the character's goals and with the character's relationship to the other characters?

The following chapters discuss the task of building cohesive characters who are able to make plot and storyline understandable and exciting to the viewer. After all, it is the director's and the actor's responsibility to work together to create living, breathing, loving and hating characters on screen.

5.1 The Complex Character And The Simple Character

THE COMPLEX CHARACTER

The *Complex Character* is fascinating, not only for the viewer to observe but for the director and the actor to create. A well-written Complex Character can give your film a decided edge. Complex Characters come in many emotional shapes. For example, in a psychodrama, a Complex Character who is important to the story's narrative may be the star, co-star or even a supporting player. But don't mistakenly overpopulate your film with them. Whether or not you create a Complex Character should be based on the character's need, not upon the so-called "effectiveness" of the role.

As already mentioned in 2.7, "Getting To Know The Characters," a Complex Character shows a Dominant Trait, a Contradictory Trait (the two should oppose each other) and possibly Supporting Traits. Let's study the character of Annie Wilkes (portrayed by Kathy Bates) in the film *Misery* (Columbia, 1990; Rob Reiner, 107 mins.). Annie Wilkes, a lonely woman living out in the country, finds a traffic accident victim. Taking him into her house and nursing him back to health, she falls in love with him and—consequently—makes him her prisoner. Her traits are listed below:

Dominant Trait	Supporting Trait
Low Self-Esteem	Shyness
Contradictory Trait	Supporting Trait
Deviousness	Cruelty

Her character constantly shifts throughout this movie, creating a fascinating character study for the viewer. As in the character of Annie Wilkes, an interesting combination of traits often leads to a well-executed performance. Consider the following various combination of traits:

- A scene dominated by Dominant Trait but glimpses of Contradictory Trait are visible: Annie Wilkes' prospective prisoner wakes up. She welcomes him into her home;
- A scene dominated by a combination of Dominant Trait and Supporting trait: Annie Wilkes and her prisoner eat supper together;
- A scene dominated either by Dominant Trait or Supporting trait: Annie Wilkes and her prisoner have their first heart-to-heart talk. She insinuates that she is in love with him;
- A scene dominated by Contradictory trait: Kathy finds out her prisoner tried to escape;
- The beginning of a scene is dominated by Dominant trait, while the conclusion of the scene is dominated by contradictory trait: Annie Wilkes tells her prisoner she will never let him leave, she'd rather kill him.

In the framework of any relationship, *Pattern Traits* often come into play. For example, in Character A, a Dominant Trait rules; in Character B, it is a Contradictory Trait; Characters C and D suffer Supporting Traits. Let's look at the character of Blanche DuBois in the television version of Tennessee Williams' play, *A Streetcar Named Desire* (Keith Barish Productions, 1984, John Erman) In this version, Ann-Margret played the role of Blanche.

Blanche Du Bois		
Dominant Trait	Self-Delusion	Controls her relationship to Stella and Mitch.
Supporting Trait	Grandeur	Controls her relationship to Stanley.
Contradictory Trait	Kind concern	Controls her relationship to Stella.
Supporting Trait	Fear	Controls her relationship to Stanley

Exercise

Select a Main Character from one of your favorite films. Then,

- Make a list of the character's traits;
- Write a list of traits illuminating this character's relationship to other characters;
- Decide which traits dominate specific scenes.

CATEGORY TYPES

Be careful when having your Complex Character come alive via *attitudes* and / or *mannerisms* (i.e., a SHY CHARACTER does not have to stutter, own a vague smile or tilt his head submissively). This can lead you and your actor down the Primrose Path to stereotyping. Therefore, before selecting certain mannerisms, you must decide whether this character is an *Extrovert* or *Introvert*. For this, we will follow noted psychologist Carl Jung's type categories:

THE EXTROVERT

Also called the *Sensational Type,* this is a character everyone loves to be with because he is outgoing, charming, talkative, sexy. The Sensational Type enjoys life through his senses. His lifelines may include good clothes, high-quality travel and entertainment. The Sensational Type can be selfish and cold if his demands are not met immediately. This type is driven by his highly developed desire for power.

THE INTROVERT

Known as the *Feeling Type*, this is a character who often is warm and loving and lives to nurture others, finding reward in helping a loved one reach success. In his own self-effacing manner, this character is socially successful. However, this type often lacks the confidence to set a goal for himself. And, believing in the best in everyone, he unfortunately is apt to be used by others.

Introvert sub-types combine characteristics, such as:

The Thinking Type. He is usually a loner. Living in a world of logic, deliberation and thought, this character type pulls away from relationships because concepts are more important than people.

The Intuitive Type is a dreamer who relies on hunches; strangely enough, he often finds that these hunches come true. (Scientists fall into this category.) The Intuitive Type relates to others as either a Feeling or Thinking Type.

All of us are type combinations. It is the Dominant Trait that determines whether a character is an Extrovert or Introvert; Supporting Traits and Contradictory Traits bring shading to the characters.

Examples

An honest, nice guy
Dominant Trait: Charm (Extrovert)
Supporting Trait: Nurturing (Introvert/Feeling Type)
By changing his Supporting Trait and adding a Contradictory Trait, look how this "honest, nice guy" changes.

Dominant Trait: Charm (Extrovert)
Supporting Trait: Determination (Extrovert)
Contradictory Trait: Thought-oriented
(Introvert/Thinking Type)
This character not only gets what he wants, but he
probably uses people. He hides his selfish motives
behind the Extrovert's mask.

Once you ensure that a strong Dominant Trait is juxtaposed against a Contradictory Trait, subtly foreshadow the Contradictory Trait. For example, if lovable, straitlaced Aunt Minnie is a kleptomaniac, show a glimpse of this affliction long before her thievery becomes a major plot point. (For example, Minnie and Clyde, her husband of 30 years, are dining out. After Clyde leaves a tip and walks away from the table, Minnie scoops the tip into her purse.)

If you need to create an offbeat character, one who "marches to the beat of his own drummer," study characteristics of abnormal behavior. The following are examples of *Abnormal Extroverted Behavior*:

- *The Manic.* Usually displaying Extrovert characteristics at an abnormally high level, the Manic lives in a world of Euphoria. Selfish to the extreme, manics care little for others and are given to emotional outbursts.
- *The Paranoid.* He is convinced that others are out to "get him" and is driven by an unreasonable need to control others. Paranoids are also arrogant and boastful.
- *The Psychopath* is completely amoral, with no understanding of right and wrong.
- *The Sociopath* is emotionally unbalanced, showing strong anti-social tendencies. The Sociopath tends to hurt those closest to him.

Within the boundaries of *Abnormal Introverted Behavior* are the following categories:

- *The Depressive.* He is tortured by extremely low self-esteem, blaming himself constantly, though he is not always at fault.
- *The Manic-Depressive* (Bi-Polar) suffers periods of euphoria interchanged with dark moods. At times, the Manic-Depressive is completely uncommunicative.
- *The Schizophrenic.* Overly sensitive, the Schizophrenic has trouble communicating with others and usually withdraws from relationships.
- *The Anxiety-Neurotic* worries about EVERYTHING.

  Before you and your actor create any character—Complex or Simple (discussed in the next segment)—ask yourselves these questions:
- What is the character's importance, relative to the plot?
- What is the character's importance, relative to the theme?
- Is the character one of the story's instigating elements?
- What is the character's relationship to other characters?
- What is his Character Type? (It must be interesting.)
- What is his Trait(s)? (It must be definite.)
- What is his Goal/Need? (It must be strong and believable.)
- What are his Attitudes? (They must be specific.)

<u>Exercise</u>

Categorize the following characters:
- Annie Wilkes (*Misery*)
- Al Pacino (*Dog Day Afternoon*)
- Richard Nixon, (*Nixon* , Touchstone, 1995; Oliver Stone, 190 mins.).

THE SIMPLE CHARACTER

The Simple Character is not limited to a supporting or an episodic role. On the contrary, it may be your bankable star who exemplifies the Simple Character in your film. Often, "star-vehicle" scripts are written to "fit" a star since it is that star's *charisma* that is designed to carry the film.

Charisma is not a special talent that makes one actor a star and another equally skilled actor a bit player; charisma has little to do with physical beauty; charisma cannot be had via a costly publicity campaign. *Charisma pertains to the viewer's purely subconscious response to an actor.* For example, the viewer may admire a quality, such as bravery or cleverness, that the actor projects—a quality the viewer himself craves. Even more importantly, the viewer perceives a sense of that actor's vulnerable trait (i.e., low self-esteem) and forms a symbiotic relationship with him, based on his own negative character trait. This subconscious connection explains the immense popularity of some actors and the lasting power of those stars who died long ago, such as Judy Garland, Elvis Presley, Marilyn Monroe and James Dean.

Therefore, never take the creation of a Simple Character easily. Never cast an actor because he looks the part. Don't direct the Simple Character like a stock stereotype. Most significantly, develop the Simple Characters in your film as carefully and with as much detail as you did the Complex

Characters. After all, it is the Simple Character who will most likely provide the obstacle that the Complex Character must struggle to overcome.

Within the framework of the Simple Character's limited but strong characteristics, define specific conditions. But, beware of clichés. Nowadays, such hyperbolized characters such as Falstaff or Tartuffe are less interesting than average human beings with definite—but believable—characteristics. (In fact, these believable characteristics often propel average characters to hilarious actions.)

The Simple Character should display clearly-defined attitudes. For example, say there are two characters (Andrew and Alistair) who are both described as Introvert/Thinking Types, both with the same Dominant Trait of analytical self-absorption. Upon closer inspection, both show completely different *attitudes and mannerisms.*

ANDREW	ALISTAIR
bookish	skeptical
fidgety	sullen
shy smile	doesn't like being touched
overly polite	avoids eye contact

Therefore, every Simple Character needs to be researched as thoroughly (i.e., with "Facts and Assumptions") as the Complex Character.

5.2 The Sensitive Actor
And The Less Sensitive Actor

THE SENSITIVE ACTOR

The term, Sensitive Actor, has come to mean an actor who is skilled at his craft while the term, Less Sensitive Actor, connotes one who is less skilled. *This is inaccurate!* The Less Sensitive Actor is not less skilled, less creative or less effective on screen. The label, Sensitive Actor, simply means that this actor has been taught *Substitution* and uses this tool effectively for his screen (and / or stage) performances. Substitution enables an actor to:

- Project emotions simply and honestly;
- React realistically to situations he has not experienced;
- Show emotions he has not experienced.

SUBSTITUTION / RELEASE OBJECT

As contradictory as it sounds, Substitution keeps the actor from thinking about his own feelings, creating instead strong and believable emotions. Stanislavski explained it this way, "Don't make feelings to order, but forget about them altogether." In other words, feelings (emotions) should never be forced and therefore projected, but, rather, they should happen automatically, as in life. Substitution is based on Stanislavski's *Sense Memories*, or the utilization of the five senses: *Touch; Smell; Sight; Sound; Taste.*

The actor *creates* an *abstract object* (the Release Object) that, when juxtaposed against one of his senses, *will automatically and instantaneously call forth the required emotion* . . .

Unfortunately, a great many directors and actors still base their method of Substitution on Stanislavski's theory of *Effective Memory*.

Effective Memory. This method requires the actor to recall a real-life, highly-emotional experience in order to juxtapose that memory with the scene to be performed. For years, actors struggled with this concept. Finally, psychologists came to the logical conclusion that Effective Memory is not usually successful because of two simple facts:

- In retrospect, emotions change. What once was a deeply affecting memory later seems less significant.
- If the actor is so traumatized by a specific recalled memory, he—in a subconscious effort to keep from being traumatized again—will be unable to recreate any emotion related to that event.

Under the time constraints of creating a performance on the set, it can be difficult for an actor to emote by first recalling a particular event and then distilling the required emotion from his Sense Memories. Under the pressure of "on-the-spot" emoting, many actors may end up performing clichéd emotions viewers have already seen many times on screen.

Although the methods of Substitution/Release Object sound complicated, it isn't and the Sensitive Actor usually has no problem utilizing it. For example, a scene you're directing may require strong and sudden fear. Do not have your actor use Effective Memory by asking him, "Remember the day you were nearly hit by a car?" Instead, ask him to name a Release Object that can create the same rush of fear; it may be from any number of suggestions, i.e., unsuspectingly touching a rattlesnake (Touch); hearing an explosion (Sound); watching a raging buffalo get close (Sight).

Let's say your actor is portraying a witness in a court case. In the scene you're about to shoot, the prosecuting attorney's questions are supposed to frighten him.

- DO NOT have the actor go back to Effective Memory of one of his own dramatic experiences. (Remember, he does not need to find a situation similar to the one the character finds himself in.)
- DO CHOOSE one of the following Release Objects, depending upon the character's reaction: SUDDEN FEAR (touching a snake or tarantula); FEAR THAT CREEPS UP, becoming stronger and more frightening (hearing a bear prowl around outside).

If the actor cannot express the required emotion honestly, don't give up. Consider that:

- The chosen Release Object is too literal.
- The actor's own emotion differs from the character's emotion (that is demanded by you and by the script).

Let me further illustrate this point. One of the films I directed (*The Red Satchel*) required a highly emotional scene in which the character looks at the New York skyline. According to the script, the character was to show exhilaration. The actress, who loved New York, naturally choose as her Release Object, the New York skyline at night (Sight). However, during take after take, her exhilarations were phony. The more takes we shot, the worse her performance became. Finally, she hit upon a different (and positively NOT LITERAL) Release Object—petting her cat (Touch)—and it worked! Her Close Up was immensely touching and believable. And while her true emotion did not express exhilaration, it did project tenderness—a far better choice than the script had required.

This example demonstrates the importance of *Particularization*. When an actor is attempting to create an emotion, a generality won't do: his needs, goals, obstacles, relationship to others should always be particularized.

As your actors use the Release Object acting tool, make sure they don't simply imagine it—or worse—think about the object; they should actually experience the object via touch, smell, sight, sound or taste.

The following exercise may help introduce your actor to the Substitution and Release Object acting tools. First, explain that this exercise is to acquaint him to Release Object only; in no way is this exercise supposed to evoke any emotion.

Exercise

Ask your actor to *select an object* with no emotional connotation. (Effective practice objects are items used everyday, such as a coffee mug, bar of soap, etc.) Once he has decided upon an object, ask him to *close his eyes*. He should relax completely; yawn; feel the tension flow from his fingertips and toes.

He should try not to think. Instead, he should *listen to the sounds* surrounding him, but not hold on to any of them. Keeping his eyes closed, he should *see the chosen object (Release Object)* suspended in front of him and make out its shape and color.

Keeping the Release Object suspended, he should lift his hands and, with his fingertips, touch and explore the object. Is it sharp? Smooth? Does it have nooks or crannies?

After a time, he should open his eyes. Now, ask him how realistic the object became.

To some actors, the object may become unbelievably real; to others, it may be inconsistent; and a number actors (the less sensitive ones) fail to experience any sensation altogether. Ask your actors to practice this exercise. After awhile, utilizing Release Objects will become second nature.

The actor following the Release Object's lead ought to permit the object to take over; he should not concentrate on the spoken lines, but rather on the physical sensation evoked by the object (Touch, Smell, Sight, Taste, Sound). Or, in other words, the *physical sensation* should give expression to the spoken lines.

However, here are a few caveats:

- Once the chosen Release Object has become real enough to evoke emotion, the actor must refrain from forcing an even higher or more flamboyant emotion.
- Do not ask any actor to perform an entire scene based on a continuous succession of Release Objects. (Getting mired in Release Objects may cause the actor to separate himself from other characters and from the situation.)
- Release Objects are for special moments only—those moments when the actor must express a deeply felt emotion or an emotion he has never experienced.

As disappointing as it may sound, Substitution cannot be used to place the image of another person over the reality of the actor's partner. For example, say you must film a tender love scene between your leading actors, Ella and Tim. As everyone on the crew already knows, Tim, is an obnoxious idiot. Intending to help, you take Ella aside and tell her to Substitute her handsome husband Ned for the obnoxious Tim. So, when she must kiss Tim, she is actually kissing Ned. Unfortunately, your well-intentioned advice is wrong! One cannot substitute a different person for the one he is playing against. Ella would do better to select a Release Object that evokes in her the emotion of tenderness needed for this scene.

Do not confuse an emotion evoked by a Release Object with *mood*. Don't push your actor into getting "in the mood" because expressing a mood usually results in ambiguous acting. Remember: When an actor must evoke an emotion in relation to his character's goals, obstacles, environment, situation and/or relationship, *Substitution (Release Object) requires clear particularization*. For example, a character named Herb is exhausted. If the actor portraying Herb "acts" tired, he comes across as phony. However, the Release Object of Touch—carrying a heavy load—can provide the actor with the required physical condition.

Be sure to ask your actor to take his time when dealing with Release Objects:

- He should not rush as he sets the Release Object;
- He should let the Release Object affect him;
- Only then should he speak his lines.

Remind your actors always to thrive for *simplicity*. Just as you should never accept one-dimensional mumbling for emotion, nor should you permit any actor to substitute seemingly effective—but false—emotions for honest ones. Remember: simplicity is depth.

Regardless what the script demands, the actor should never attempt to show emotions he does not feel, or is unable to arouse via a Release Object. In addition, many times a skilled, creative actor mistakes a laissez-faire, monotonous acting style, for natural on-screen acting. For instance, the actor slouches, mumbles, and though claiming he feels every emotional aspect the character is supposed to show, mumbling and showing no trace of emotion, he disconnects from the character, from the purpose of the scene and from the script's overall demand. This type of acting is dull and also tends to fog up the plot's narrative line. The use of Substitution pulls the actor away from this kind of generalizing performance.

THE LESS SENSITIVE ACTOR

Do not confuse the *Less Sensitive Actor* with the *Simple Character*. The first term refers to the ACTOR'S *emotional makeup*; the second to the characterization of the ROLE. (Some may classify the Sensitive Actor as a "Feeling" Type, while the Less Sensitive Actor might be classified as a "Thinking" Type.) Therefore, while your work with the Sensitive Actor, you may focus primarily on his character's inner life and relationship with others, your work with the Less Sensitive Actor may evolve around goal-related elements: establishing the GOAL; taking ACTION toward that goal; the PHYSICALIZATION of that action.

THE GOAL

Once the character's goal has been established, it must be stated clearly. Although the goal is as important for the Sensitive Actor as for the Less Sensitive Actor, it is the Less Sensitive Actor whose creative powers are nourished by it.

Example

Situation: Ralph wants to take over Tom's job.

```
INT. BREAK ROOM—DAY

Ralph, sitting at a table, a cup of coffee
in front of him, talking to a coworker.

                RALPH
          I've got to take over
          Tom's job. The guy is
          getting old and fuzzy—you
          should've heard that
          telephone conversation he
          had with our supplier—
          pure mush. Anyway, it
          will be better for the
          firm if I were to sit at
          Tom's desk. Ya get my
          drift.
```

The actor portraying Ralph should take a close look at this dialogue, explaining his character's goal, and *particularize* it from there. He should:

- Narrow Ralph's goal to a simple: I WANT TO.
- Continue it with action words—TAKE OVER. "I WANT TO TAKE OVER."
- Still too general, we need to know HOW Ralph intends to take over. This particularization of HOW relates to Ralph's established Character Type and Traits:

Statement	Character Type	Dominant Trait
"I want to FORCE my way in."	Extrovert	Forceful determination
"I want to CLAW my way in."	Extrovert	Forceful determination, with a trace of mania
"I want to SWEET TALK my way in."	Extrovert	Charm (Supportive Trait: Deviousness)
"I want to FIND discriminating evidence against Tom."	Introvert	Thinking Type

Once the character's goal has been set according to his personality, you and the actor must search for the goal's subconscious reason, or, the character's *need* (where the strongest goals are rooted). Most likely, such needs are not spelled out in the script. It is the responsibility of you and your actor to delve beneath the written word to uncover the ONE need that is sympathetic with the character's personality.

If Ralph Says . . .	His Need Is . . .
"I NEED a better paying job."	Ralph's child support is overdue; he loves his child and wants to GIVE HIM THE BEST.
"I NEED a more prestigious position."	Ralph wants to BOLSTER his low self-esteem.
"I NEED more responsibility."	Ralph is bored with his job; he needs a CHALLENGE.

Exercise

Study the film, *Fiddler On The Roof* (United Artists, 1971; Norman Jewison, 184 mins.) Select three scenes, then decide upon Tevye's goals in each.

THE ACTIONS

The particularization of the character's goal [WHAT DOES HE WANT OR NEED] leads to his subgoals [HOW DOES HE GET WHAT HE WANTS] in mental and physical actions. Subgoals form part of a script's plot, but it is your job, as director, to stress areas that support the appropriate subgoals.

Example

Ralph attends a company board meeting, during which he has only a few unimportant lines. Without paying attention to Ralph's subgoals, the actor may turn in a perfunctory performance, brushing off his lines. Ralph's goal, however, as established previously, is: I WANT TO TAKE OVER. It will be intensified by his subgoal: I WANT TO BUILD A NETWORK OF SUPPORTERS. Therefore, the actor can express Ralph's subgoal via physical actions.

> Whenever the company president speaks, Ralph nods approvingly. [I WANT TO MAKE MYSELF VALUABLE TO THE MOVERS AND SHAKERS.]
>
> Ralph takes copious notes. [I WANT TO MAKE MYSELF MORE IMPORTANT.]

Never consider physical actions unimportant. In addition, do not permit the actor to move about the scene haphazardly. Whenever a physical action is to be performed, the actor must decide:

- Why [*mental*] is the character doing this physical activity?
- How [*physical*] is the character doing this activity?

<u>Example</u>

Amy does the dishes. The actress playing Amy should ask herself:

- *Why am I doing this physical activity?*

<u>Amy's Mental Action</u>

```
                AMY
            (to herself)
    I shouldn't do these
    dirty dishes. Tonight is
    Rick's turn to wash up
    but that lazy bum fell
    asleep, as always, in
    front of the TV. And what
    does he do all day? He
    sits in his office and
    makes calls, takes cli-
    ents to lunch. Big deal.
    I never go out to fancy
    places. I sit at home, I
    take care of screaming
    kids, I cook, I clean the
    house, I do laundry ..."
```

Then, still as Amy, the actress should ask herself:
- *How am I doing this physical activity?*

Amy's Physical Action

Angrily, Amy bangs pots and pans around the kitchen.

Amy's Goal:

I WANT TO SHOW RICK HOW FURIOUS I AM.

As director, you must make the actor aware of the character's circumstance at all times because, at any given moment, the character might be observant, tired, restless, relaxed, anticipating, etc. As a result, the opportunities for the character to perform honest and simple physical actions are countless.

Exercise

Study *Fiddler On The Roof* one more time. Then,
- Decide whether Tevye's physical actions are in harmony with or in contrast to the goals you had established during the previous exercise.
- Compare the goals and physical actions shown in *Fiddler On The Roof* to those in *The First Wives Club* (Paramount, 1996, Hugh Wilson). When correlating the characters' goals and physical actions, which film is more effective?

HELPFUL HINTS

Following are some helpful hints you may want to share with your actors before shooting begins:
- Once you have called, "Action!" your actor should not start the scene (dialogue and/or physical action)

immediately. Instead, he should silently count ("1001, 1002") before commencing activity. Without this quiet moment, it is almost impossible for the editor to cut from one take to the next.

- Walking in a Two-Shot (with the camera moving in front of the actors), your actor should not start his lines when he takes his first step, i.e., if he must say the following line, "And then we went to New York," it would be choreographed like this:

Spoken line: "And..."

Start walking as he says, "...we went to New York."

- In a seated or standing Two-Shot (the actors are looking at each other), do not permit a "nose-to-nose" position; rather, move each of their faces to a 45° angle.

- If, within the perimeter of the walking Two-Shot, actors turn and face each other, have each look into the other's eye that is closest to the camera.

- Remind your actors to slightly slow down any physical action because the camera sees movements faster than does the human eye.

5.3 Dialogue

Although contradictory in nature, a script's dialogue is not created to be spoken, but to be read. After all, those interested in financing or distributing your film READ the script; they do not act it out. In fact, you probably had few qualms about the way the characters communicated with each other during your initial script analysis phase (see Part 2, "Introduction"). But as you hear actors speak the dialogue, you might notice some lines sounding stilted and/or unnatural. Truthfully, in every script, some dialogue should be changed. But, don't worry: dialogue changes are normal and everyone expects them, which is the reason the writer often is (and should be) present during production. If not, it becomes YOUR job to change dialogue where appropriate. Of course, your actors will have suggestions and you should listen to them. However, accept the changes you like and forget the rest.

Dialogue changes will not be difficult if you keep a few basic points in mind:

- The best dialogue consists of short exchanges (i.e., give and take) between characters.
- If one character is partial to monologues, divide his overly long text between partners, or (if this doesn't serve the scene) have a partner(s) interrupt by asking questions or making comments.
- Be certain that dialogue reveals character.
- Be aware that characters have different speech patterns.
- Dialogue is not always necessary: at times, thoughts or physical actions can reveal character or situation more clearly than the spoken word.

THE GOAL

Simply and clearly, explain each character's goal. If possible, base character goals upon *need*.

THE OBSTACLE

Clarify the obstacles each character must overcome. Make certain that whatever method a character uses to overcome his obstacle, it is rooted in his character traits.

THOUGHTS

In life, people do not speak in grammatically correct, complete sentences as taught by English professors. Usually, we skip around or change topics in midstream; we ask questions; we don't finish sentences; in short we do not "converse," we TALK. Most importantly, our "talking" is always laced with emotions and thought.

- Emotion leads to thought, which leads to speech.

  Thought:

  > "I love you."

  Spoken Line:

  > "I love you."

- Thought may be stronger than a spoken line.

  Thought:

  > "I love you so much it
  > hurts, but I'm afraid to
  > tell you."

  Spoken Line:

  > "I think we're getting
  > along pretty well...."

- Thought may be opposite that of spoken lines.

Thought:

```
"If I don't propose to
you, you little fool, I'm
going to lose my inherit-
ance. So, here goes...."
```

Spoken Line:

```
"I love you."
```

Actors should always be aware that *thought* may happen at any time:

Before a Line:

```
"I've got to say it."
```

In the Middle of a Line:

```
"I...[THOUGHT: here it
goes]...love you."
```

After a Line:

```
"I love you." [THOUGHT:
Great Scot! I've said
it.]
```

Thoughts, same as spoken lines, can be expressed positively or negatively, but in both cases, the dialogue should be "readable" to the viewer. There is a scene in *Arthur* (Warner Bros., 1981; Steve Gordon, 97 mins.) when Arthur (portrayed by Dudley Moore) is forced by his father to get married; this scene is an excellent example of the integration of Thought/Spoken Lines explained above.

Thoughts, expressed in a visually interesting way, will be your lifesaver during the editing process.

Example

An actor has been saddled with a long but necessary expository speech (i.e., ". . . a monster ten feet tall, all covered with slime, was discovered in Aunt Mathilda's drawing room . . ." etc.).

Every so often, cut to the listener's expression and his THOUGHTS, voicing over (VO) the actor's lines.

In reversals, you should cut from one actor's reaction to his partner's reaction.

TARGETS

Thoughts, especially in a tight Two-Shot or Close Up, should be made visibly interesting via *targets,* which are points of focus for thoughts and/or spoken lines. The process of targeting brings forth thoughts and illuminates the spoken word; it never turns an actor into a computerized image or restricts his emotions. All people target when they talk. (Have you ever spoken to another without moving your eyes or your head?)

Targeting can be filmed from three points of view:

- When the actor targets *Another Person*: He looks at his scene partner. If in a Close Up and/or reversal shot, he looks at the camera.
- When the actor targets *Himself*: He looks down.
- When the actor targets *What He Thinks or Speaks About*: He looks to the side.

These targets, as mechanical as they seem, are what we use automatically in everyday communications. (Watch people conversing and you will agree.) Targets, if not overused, make spoken lines come alive. But beware: the actor's movement should be natural while he is targeting.

Targets are especially helpful for the actor when emoting what lines do not express.

Example

An actor must utter the following line: "Yesterday, I saw your girlfriend at the club."

The line, by itself, has no significance: Character A sees Character B's girlfriend at the tennis club. *See* how the line's significance changes if delivered via *targeting*:

Target: Another Person

```
"Yesterday, I saw your
girlfriend at the club."
```

Target: Himself

```
"Yesterday, I saw your
girlfriend at the club."
```

Target: What He Thinks or Speaks About

```
"Yesterday, I saw your
girlfriend at the club."
```

The targets, indicating some hesitancy on the actor's part, make the viewer wonder what's going on.

Exercise

Restudy *Fiddler On The Roof.* Now, remembering back to the Goal and Physical Action segments discussed earlier, examine the way Tevye (portrayed by Topol) connects physical actions and lines with THOUGHT. Watch the way Topol targets.

COMMUNICATION LEVELS

You have worked diligently on the script's intensity and communication levels. Now, it is time to make sure that these elements do not get lost during principal photography. Be sure to keep a tight rein on communication levels. Don't accept any performance that, though interesting, is detrimental to the film's narrative line. Watch out for:

- Interrelationships between characters;
- Interrelationships between characters and environment;
- Communication levels between characters;
- Which character will dominate in which scenes;
- The Apex scene being emotionally, visually or verbally expressed (it is important to remember that camera setups and movements often depend on Apex);
- The variation of intensity levels from scene to scene.

RHYTHM AND PACING

Remember Rhythm and Pacing from the script analysis? As a refresher, the visual aspects *Rhythm* affects a character from the outside while *Pace* affects a character emotionally, that is to say, from the inside.

This acting tool originated at the Moscow Art Theater during the turn of the century. The concept of Rhythm and Pacing is important for modern-day motion picture directors because, since this concept is based upon the interaction of physical and mental conditions, it determines a character's physical actions. Following are the degrees of action, as established by the Moscow Art Theater:

1. A person close to death;
2. A person fatigued from illness or exhaustion;
3. A tired or sad person;
4. A mentally slow person;
5. The normal, everyday pace of the average, emotionally sound and healthy person;
6. A nervous person;

7. A tense, angry person;
8. A person afraid of losing control;
9. A person falling apart;
10. A psychotic person.

ENVIRONMENT

The influence of environment (place and time) upon characters should be one of your main concerns. As discussed in 2.2, "Impact of the Environment," environment includes the location where the character had been previous to the current scene, or where the character will be going in the following scene. Even if pressed for time, you should clarify the environment for your actor by having him answer these questions:

- Where am I?
- Where was I before and what did I do there?
- Where will I be going next?
- What time of the day is it?
- Is there anything outstanding, comforting, frightening, bizarre, etc., in the environment?
- How do I feel physically?
- How do I feel emotionally?
- How does the clothing feel on my body?
- What is the Rhythm and Pacing pattern for the current scene?

During production, it is not easy for the director to adjust the environment to please an actor-character's physical or emotional condition. (Following Murphy's Law, most beach scenes will be shot on cold winter days; and if your film takes place in Antarctica, don't be surprised if most of the exterior scenes are shot on a sound stage, when actors are costumed in heavy winter clothing while it is 90° outside and the crew works wearing T-shirts and shorts!)

Often, actors must project physical conditions they have not experienced naturally. If you rehearse the cast prior to principal photography, you'll have the chance to introduce them to the technique of Substitution/Release Object. For "on set" rehearsals, you may have to opt for a generalized *Physical Projection*. Let's compare Release Object and Physical Projection with the most common reactions to our environment:

IN COMPARISON TO:	RELEASE OBJECT	PHYSICAL PROJECTION
COLD	Feel ice slide down your spine	Clutch your elbows and rub your arms
HEAT	Feel heavy load on your shoulders, which gets heavier with each step.	Your breathing is shallow and your head is bent down
FEAR	Ants crawling up your spine and in the palm of your hand	Hunch your shoulders
COMFORT	A warm glow radiating from your solar plexus.	Feel relaxed all over.

MOTIVE AND REACTION

A motive should always precede a character's reaction; it should be strong enough to be recognized by the viewer; the actor's reaction should be appropriate to the situation. On a more subliminal level, Motive-Reaction affects the viewer's subconscious reaction to the events shown on the screen.

The *symbolism of the visual elements* should be your main concern as you decide whether to emphasize spoken or visual elements.

<u>Example</u>

Mary and Joe are going to be married the next day.

Emphasis on the spoken word: Cuddled together on a sun-kissed meadow, they talk about the happy future ahead of them.

Visual Elements in Accordance with Spoken Word: Camera movements express the young couple's happiness, i.e., high grasses, sun-drenched backdrop; a brook murmurs its congratulations; trees protect the lovers. *The dialogue has become negligible.*

Visual elements in Juxtaposition with Spoken Word: Tree branches threateningly reach up to the cloud-laden sky. Grasses, at first motionless, have turned to sharp daggers. *The dialogue achieves an eerie quality as it stands in strong opposition to the visual elements shown.*

5.4 The Director And The "Star"

Rarely will a director cast the star of his own film. Usually, the production and / or distribution company financing the project decides who should star. Often a script has been developed and written with a certain star in mind. However, if a script has not been written for a specific star, it usually doesn't matter whether the selected star is right for the part: all that matters is the star's box-office appeal.

Box-office draw is power—that's a fact of life every director must live with. The film industry is fortunate to be blessed with many stars who not only have looks, personality and name appeal, but who are also terrific actors. Yet, for the standard commercial film, most directors must deal with the "The Personality," or, "The Simple Character" star.

THE PERSONALITY, OR, THE SIMPLE CHARACTER STAR

There is nothing wrong with the Simple Character star if the director supports the star with gripping visuals and with a cast that enhances the star's personality. In addition, the characters supporting the star must be *clearly delineated*. Be careful that none of the supporting roles projects a personality or trait similar to that of the star. And don't forget to illuminate the lead actor's STAR QUALITY—his charisma.

Study the film, *Goldeneye* (MGM, 1995; Martin Campbell, 130 mins.), starring Pierce Brosnan, for an excellent example of the Simple Character Star.

THE FLAT STAR

Working with the Flat Star requires the director's ingenuity because this kind of star most likely delivers lines in a monotone or in a clichéd way. Keep his lines short and surround him with a carefully selected cast, but give him all the on-screen time he deserves, he is the one who draws the audience to the theater.

5.5 The Director
And The Casting Process

If you are directing a film for a Screen Actor's Guild (SAG) signatory company, the production company's *Casting Director* will send to the Breakdown Service a list of roles to be cast. All SAG-franchised (SAG-approved) agencies subscribe to the Breakdown Service. Agencies then send their clients' 8x10 head shots and resumés to the production company's casting office.

The casting director usually is free to cast day players without the director's and/or producer's approval because, in all likelihood, the director does not work with these actors, meeting them only on the day they are scheduled to work. The Assistant Director (AD) tells the day players when and where to sit, stand or move, and when to say their lines. Usually, the day players are typecast: an actor who looks like a priest is cast as a priest; an actor who looks like a cop is cast as a cop, etc. It doesn't make a lot sense (most people we meet do not look like "types"), but this is how casting is done.

When casting for co-stars or featured players, the casting director will interview and/or "read" appropriate prospective actors. He will then introduce the director to those actors who, in his opinion, are right for the role. As director, you won't be involved with the actors' initial readings or callback readings. You might have to remember that, while all of the actors may have the right "look," there is likely to be a difference between their "look" and their acting ability.

When casting co-stars, casting directors might suggest actors who are known and have a solid background of film work, or actors who are television stars; some casting directors attend stage plays or attend acting seminars; many casting directors depend upon the advice of agents with whom they frequently work. They rarely cast actors they meet during acting seminars. For these reasons, it is difficult for a beginning actor to gain a foothold in the industry.

If you are directing a non-union film (the production company is not a SAG signatory) you and your producer will share the casting responsibilities. Forget about listing your production with the Breakdown Service; forget about contacting agencies. Theatrical agencies submitting clients for feature and television work represent SAG actors exclusively. They submit non-union actors for non-union COMMERCIALS only. In fact, any production company not a signatory with SAG is prohibited from casting SAG actors. On the other hand, the producer of a SAG signatory film cannot cast union AND non-union actors for the same production. However, a producer can hire a non-union actor if the production company:

- Guarantees the actor a minimum of three days work in a speaking role;
- Obtains a SAG membership for the actor; the actor pays the SAG initiation fee and dues.

If you have been signed to direct a non-union film and you are located in the Los Angeles area, send your casting notices to:

DramaLogue
1456 North Gordon Avenue
Los Angeles, CA 90028

In the New York area you may want to contact:

Back Stage
1515 Broadway
New York, NY 10036-8986

If you are shooting outside of these major motion picture areas, it might be best to contact the Telecommunications and / or Drama Department at the local college. If your local college doesn't have a Drama Department, try a local theater group.

Be sure to look for actors who have *on screen* experience (even a student film will do). It is difficult to work with actors who have no professional experience, but semi-professional actors probably will be fine in day-player roles.

Regardless where you submit your casting notices, expect to be buried under an avalanche of 8x10 head shots! When you begin wading through these submissions, don't be too particular: set aside head shots of actors you think might do; don't look for perfect character types because photos can be misleading. Stay away from non-actors, or your enthusiastic friends or relatives who think making a film is "fun." When directing a documentary, if the look is perfect, a non-actor usually is fine. THIS IS NOT TRUE WHEN DIRECTING A FEATURE FILM! Even an acting coach can't get non-actors ready for the camera. As any experienced acting coach will tell you, it takes two years of teaching and experience to get an actor ready for performing on stage or on screen.

Once you have a stack of photos you are interested in, it's time to read their attached resumés. Don't be swayed by actors who, though not yet members of SAG, show a long list of impressive feature film and / or television credits. The actors may have worked on these productions, but in all likelihood, they worked as Extras (*Atmosphere*). Unfortunately, extras work does not count for acting experience, nor does it guarantee acting skills. Do look for the following actors who have:

- The look and who are within the desired age group (give this some leeway and consider actors who do not quite fit the image you have formed).
- Non-union feature film credits, student film experience or have studied on-camera techniques with an acting coach.

Regardless how skilled or creative an actor might be, he should not be considered unless he has some on-screen experience and/or training. For leading and/or co-starring roles, don't cast any actor who has only stage experience. (Watching the stage actor on screen will be an unpleasant surprise because he has been trained to project emotions to the audience. Conversely, the film actor has been taught to pull the viewer into the events on the screen.) Granted, the experienced stage actor's first reading might be impressive: he may give you a flamboyant picture of how his character should be portrayed. But, usually, this flamboyance does not come across on film the same way. In addition, because of his training and experience, the stage actor will feel uncomfortable in front of the camera, which puts restrictions on him. Unlike stage acting, the film actor is prohibited from moving freely, from using extensive hand and head gestures; he must repeat the same lines over and over; he must hit marks; and, most disconcertingly, when filming Two-Shots and Reversals, he does not receive any visual response from his partner. Consequently, the stage actor either over-projects or turns in a one-dimensional performance. Though the emotions he experiences are real enough, his performance comes across as "theatrical," and therefore phony, or stiff.

THE FIRST READING OR INTERVIEW

Don't give an actor the impression you are doing him a favor by interviewing him. In no way are you more important than he, no matter what part he is reading for. As director, you are searching for actors to be cast; actors come to you to get hired. You are on the same level. Therefore, always give actors the respect they deserve.

As the actor reads for the part, don't confuse him by bombarding him with suggestions about how the character should be portrayed. Instead, look at what the actor brings to the role. If he should ask for advice on the character, offer some guidance but suggest he interpret the character himself. Such an answer gives the actor a sense of independence and self-assurance.

During the first set of readings, you should not look for the perfect cast; rather, concern yourself with the actors who MAY be right for roles. Here are some *plus points* you should look for:

- The reading should be spontaneous and natural, but not too casual.
- The actor should not obscure or push lines.
- The actor communicates the character's opinion, goals and needs and shows honest emotions.
- The actor is relaxed.

Following are some *minus points*:

- The actor does a perfunctory "line reading," i.e., he reads the dialogue without considering the character's emotions, goals or needs.
- The actor reads in a monotonous way.
- The actor reads "theatrically," or shows emotion he doesn't relate to.
- The actor is nervous.

You'll encounter all kinds of First Readings. But, every so often, you'll be surprised by a reading that is of performance-level quality: it will be so perfect, the actor could be filmed on the spot. If you are lucky enough to find such an actor AND if he has sufficient on-camera experience, do not hesitate to cast him, whether or not he has the perfect "look." You have just uncovered a rare find.

Always suggest that actors take the *sides* with them. You may want to see some of them a second time; but, don't decide on whom to call back until you have read all applicants.

THE CALLBACK

Roughly, twenty-five percent of the actors you interview will be called back. Some of the readings at the Callback may be better this time around while others will be worse. Unfortunately, a number of talented actors don't read well during callbacks. They have diligently worked on their lines but they may have lost the immediacy they had shown during the initial reading. Such an actor won't do for your film; most likely, his performance will weaken as his lines have to be repeated during multiple takes. Other actors will retain all the positive qualities you noticed during the first reading, but will have nothing new to add. (Keep these actors in mind.) However, a few actors will have worked on the role while retaining the immediacy of their first audition and will have made the character come more alive. These are the actors you should seriously consider.

Again, don't be tempted to cast your film immediately. Be sure to check for the following points:
- Has the actor fused his own personality with that of the character?
- Has the actor made the dialogue his own, via thoughts?
- Has the actor considered the character's physical environment?

In addition, during the Callback, you can learn whether or not the actor is "directable." Give him some suggestions on how you would like the scene to be read. The actor who follows your advice without losing spontaneity or his ability to communicate will be easy to direct.

Many times, you may opt for a third or fourth Callback. (If you are casting a union film, the production company must pay for all Callbacks after the first one). It is during these extra Callbacks when you should determine:

- Do actors differ in looks and demeanor, concerning the characters they are supposed to portray?
- How well prospective cast members relate (as their characters) to one another. Do any of your actor operate in a vacuum, or is there give and take (lively interaction) between characters?

And finally, the moment of decision arrives: WHOM SHALL WE CAST? Often you'll have to decide between looks (the more handsome guy, the more beautiful girl), appropriateness to the character and charisma, versus acting ability. But remember, a choice must be made, no matter how difficult.

PART 6

THE
DIRECTOR
AND THE
LOCUSTS
OF CREATIVITY

6.1 Avoiding The Locusts

You may have worked on a film or heard of one that, although meticulously prepared, fell apart after it was completed. What happened? The dailies looked great <u>even though</u> the story strayed a bit from its original plot line; the relationships were touching <u>even though</u> they were toyed with during production. Do these elements really matter? They matter a great deal!

Beware of the *locusts of creativity*—those brilliant but sudden inspirations, those great scenes that had to be added—because these will pull your film apart. It begins so innocently: the cinematographer has a good idea; the star (aware of his self-importance) insists on a simple change; soon, every Tom, Dick and Mary chimes in. The locusts of creativity have taken over! This may happen to you any number of times. Sometimes, the filmed result of a suggestion is fantastic. However, most likely, the final result on screen will be a film that is too difficult to follow.

The director, tired of these endless suggestions, may be tempted to give in to them. Worse, you may disregard previous decisions you have made regarding your script's narrative line, suspense and character relationships. Consequently, all of the elements that are important to your film's forward movement—those you painstakingly developed with the writer—will get muddled.

Keep in mind that no film is ever shot as planned and flexibility is necessary. In fact, it is almost impossible to hold on to every scene or element that you had planned. But . . . don't open the doors to the locusts of creativity! To protect yourself, your reputation and your film, keep with you a list of your script's basic story and character relationship considerations. If faced with a barrage of creative suggestions, do not give in to anything before consulting your list—this is your *locust trap*. Consider the following trap parameters:

- Is each scene the logical outcome of the preceding one? Does each scene connect to the following one?
- Does the scene you are shooting give a *reaction* to a previously established *motive*?
- Do obstacles increase in intensity?
- Is there overlapping suspense? (Remember, all major scenes, as well as some minor ones, should place a question into the viewer's mind. The question should not be answered, creating *overlapping suspense*, until a new question has been established.)
- Is focus achieved by the logical development of plot and/or relationships? (Scenes or incidents not cogent to the plot's logic or unity should be omitted.)
- Do the *first fifteen minutes* of your film grip the viewer?
- Is there *Surprise versus Suspense*? Suspense must be established while Surprise must be sudden and unexpected. Surprise adds shock value, but don't overdo it because Suspense controls the viewer's empathy.
- Does the crisis prior to the denouement stem from an earlier conflict (dark moment) that has since been intensified?
- Is the denouement causal, i.e., is it the logical outcome of character traits and/or inter-relationships?
- Does the climax have proper buildup, or does it come too suddenly? (Generally, a series of interrelated scenes better serves the denouement than a long and involved one.)

- Have all loose ends been tied up?
- Has the main question—established at the beginning of the script—been answered clearly?
- Does the film end after the main question has been answered, or does it suffer from an anticlimax?
- Does the film show proper graduation of plot and of characters and their relationships?
- Do events, incidents and relationships overlap sufficiently?
- Do all of the events and/or situations contain dramatic logic? (Two cars chasing each other is not dramatic. However, if the viewer knows *why* the cars are chasing each other, then the action will have dramatic value.) *All actions must be motivated.*
- Have two incidents of a similar nature been avoided?
- Are obstacles and conflicts clearly delineated?
- Does the viewer know everyone? Are relationships clear?
- Does the viewer get a glimpse of a character's Contradictory Trait BEFORE this trait plays a part in the story?
- Are protagonist and antagonist clearly delineated? How about all other characters?
- Does the viewer have all necessary information regarding plot, character relationships, etc.?
- Do Complex Characters and Simple Characters retain their uniqueness, or do they fall prey to stereotypical mannerisms?
- Are characters sufficiently motivated?
- Are characters dramatically involved in the story, or do they serve as decoration?

- Do incidents and situations contain human interest? Are they filmed in a way that draws the viewer into the screen, i.e., permits the viewer to participate in the filmed event?

Though most of the above-mentioned points should have been addressed during the script analysis phase (see Part 2, "Introduction"), you should keep all of these points in mind during principal photography. Being intimately aware of the answers to these questions will help you keep the locusts at bay.

PART 7

THE
DIRECTOR'S
HOMEWORK

7.1 The Storyboard

You are probably familiar with the terms, *Breakdown Board* and *Storyboard*. There is a difference between the two.

THE BREAKDOWN BOARD

As the director, you will work in concert with the Production Manager to create individual scene breakdown sheets. Breakdown sheets for the next day's shooting schedule (which include scenes to be shot, locations, actors involved) are distributed to everyone on the production at the end of each shooting day.

The *Breakdown Board* contains the entire shooting schedule. Consisting of strips of various colors, the Breakdown Board clearly indicates which scenes (and scene numbers) will shoot on which days and at which locations. If the production schedule moves ahead quickly, or (Heaven forbid!) gets behind, the Production Manager adjusts the strips accordingly. The Breakdown Board remains in the production office.

THE STORYBOARD

The *Storyboard* is a compilation of sketches, created by a Storyboard Artist, illustrating the choreography of a scene (or sequence of scenes), according to the director's desired camera setups and movements. The Storyboard can be an immense help to the director. Considering the chaos and time pressures that are a normal part of principal photography, the Storyboard can be the life preserver that keeps the director focused and the production on schedule.

A Storyboard is usually needed whenever the original shooting script undergoes changes, or if there is a particularly difficult action sequence to film.

Some directors may sketch the drawings themselves, utilizing their own artistic talent or rudimentary form ("stick figures"). Also, there is Storyboarding software on the market, such as "Visual Walk Through."

At the beginning of your directing career, you should decide whether you prefer utilizing a detailed shooting script, a Storyboard (which you probably would have to illustrate yourself), or both.

Let's look at two versions of the following scene, broken down as if they were storyboarded:

Example

```
INT. ELMER DRAWING ROOM—DAY

Gregg enters.

                    GREGG
          Sorry to be late. Got
          caught in traffic.

                    ANNE
          Excuses, excuses.

                    GREGG
          Don't gripe. Come on.
          Let's look for it.

Gregg walks over to the fireplace. He takes
a look.

                    GREGG
                    (cont'd)
          The painting...it's
          gone...You told me...

                    ANNE
          Impossible.

The door opens a crack. Unobserved by Gregg
and Anne, ELVIRA peeks in.
```

And now, to *Storyboard Scene #1*, which places the viewer into the *Subjective Position*, or Gregg's shoes.

Storyboard Scene #1

INT. ELMER DRAWING ROOM—DAY

1 WIDE SHOT on Gregg entering.

> GREGG
>
> Sorry...

2 Camera DOLLIES IN on Gregg to a 3/4 shot.

> GREGG
> ...to be late...got...

3 Camera PANS with Gregg as he walks up to Anne.

> GREGG
> ...stuck in traffic.

Gregg, moving into a 45º profile position, stops next to Anne. Anne faces the camera.

4 Camera DOLLIES IN to tight Medium Shot.

> ANNE
> Excuses, excuses.

> GREGG
> Don't gripe. Come on...

Gregg diagonally crosses in front of Anne.

5 Camera PANS with Gregg.

> GREGG
> ...let's look for it.

6 Camera STOPS with Gregg at the fireplace. Gregg turns (open to camera).

> GREGG
> (cont'd)
> The painting...

7 Camera DOLLIES IN to Tight Medium Shot.

> GREGG
> (cont'd)
> ...it's gone...You...

Anne enters frame.

```
                    GREGG
                 (cont'd)
              ...told me...

                    ANNE
              Impossible.

    8 CUT TO door. ELVIRA peeks in.
```

The choreography for Storyboard Scene #1 is fairly simple, although it covers a relatively wide area (the Drawing Room). Since actors must hit their marks, you would coordinate the movements between camera and actor. Most likely, your DP will "soft light" this area, but two additional lighting setups will be necessary: one where Gregg meets Anne and the other during the dialogue in front of the fireplace. If you are behind schedule and must make up for lost time, the movements will need to be more simplified; the same holds true if this scene is shot in a small room rather than in a spacious drawing room.

Storyboard Scene #2 is choreographed with simple movements and puts the viewer into the omnipotent (Godlike) position.

Storyboard Scene #2

```
    INT. ELMER DRAWING ROOM—DAY

    1 Camera on Anne, a 3/4 shot.

                    GREGG
                 (VO)
              Sorry...

    Gregg enters frame.

                    GREGG
                 (cont'd)
              ...to be late.

    2 Camera DOLLIES IN to Medium Shot.

                    ANNE
              Excuses, excuses.
```

```
                       GREGG
              Don't gripe. Let's...

     Gregg crosses in front of Anne. He exits
     frame. Camera HOLDS on Anne.
                       GREGG
                    (cont'd)
                 ...look for it.

     Anne shrugs.

     3 CUT TO Loose Medium Shot, door. ELVIRA
     peeks in.

     4 CUT TO Tight Medium Shot. On Gregg,
     standing in front of the fireplace.
                       GREGG
                    (cont'd)
              The painting...it's gone.
              You told me...

     Anne enters frame.

                       ANNE
                 Impossible.
```

Aside from *time* and *place* requirements, you should consider the way the scene connects to the previous one. In the variation of the scenes depicted above, Storyboard Scene #1 is the more fluid because Gregg's lengthy dialogue scene is enlivened by actor and camera movements. However, if the preceding scene is a lively one (say, a party), featuring a lot of movement, you might prefer Storyboard Scene #2.

THE SHOT LIST

You, the production manager and the cinematographer must understand the necessity of the strict time frames demanded by the Shot List. Following are examples of Shot Lists for Storyboard Scenes #1 and #2.

SHOT LIST FOR STORYBOARD SCENE #1

7:00–8:00 am		Soft lights setup
		Rehearse actors
8:00–8:30 am		
	201	On Gregg, wide shot
	202	Dolly in on Gregg
	203	PAN with Gregg
8:30–9:00 am		Light set up, Gregg, Anne position
		Rehearse actors
9:00–9:30 am		
	204	on Gregg and Anne
	205	PAN with Gregg
9:30–10:00 am		Light set up fireplace
		Rehearse actors
10:00–10:30 am		
	206	On Gregg, camera stops
	207	Dolly, Anne enters frame
10:30–11:00 am		Light set up at door
	208	On Elvira

SHOT LIST FOR STORYBOARD SCENE #2

7:00–7:30 am		Light set up (Anne's position
		Rehearse actors
7:30–8:00 am		
	201	On Anne
	202	Dolly in on Anne and Gregg
	203	On Elvira

You and the cinematographer MUST stay within the time frame scheduled for either Shot List. If you take more time than allocated, your shooting schedule will tighten as principal photography progresses.

7.2 More Lists

The Production Manager, the Assistant Director, the Director (with assistance from the Script Supervisor) create the Scene Breakdowns for the entire script. This task must be completed long before the film begins production, as many budgetary and location decisions depend upon these breakdowns. Script Breakdown forms are available at stores specializing in the film industry such as Enterprise Stationers and Alan Gordon Enterprises in Hollywood.

Example

Scene Breakdown

Pict. No .... Set No .... Sheet No ....

Ext .... Int ....

Scene Numbers

Total Scenes................. Total Dialogue ....

No. Pages .... Day .... Night.............

Description

Gregg finds the picture has been stolen. Elvira watches.

Cast	*Wardrobe*	*Bits*
Gregg	Tuxedo	None
Anne	Evening Dress	None
Elvira	Evening Dress	None

Props	*Atmosphere*	*Music*
None	None	None

Sound Effects	*Cars, Livestock*	*Special Effects*
None	None	None

Script Supervisor

THE DIRECTOR'S CHECKLIST

The moment you call, "That's a wrap!" the shooting day ends for the cast and crew, but not for you! You still have tasks to perform. You must:

- Go over the next day's Scene Breakdown and Shot List with the Cinematographer and Production Manager.
- Confirm locations with the Production Manager.
- Review, with your Assistant Director (AD), the list of actors to be called the next day.

- Check with your Script Supervisor on the number of pages that have been shot. Is the production on schedule, or is it behind?
- Review the Daily Report with the Assistant Cameraman. Check scene numbers filmed and how much footage was shot; learn which takes are to be printed. Each film can should be clearly marked; keep a copy of this record for your file.

If the producer is actively involved in the shoot, he will take care of most of these responsibilities (you still will consult with the cinematographer about the next day's schedule), or have the production manager involved in them. However, before principal photography commences, be clear on who does what job.

PART 8

WHAT
NOW?

8.1 Your Road Map To Success

By the time you are ready to "throw yourself into the arena," others may assume that you have mastered your craft and that you are ready to compete with other—more experienced (but not necessarily more talented)—directors. You realize, of course, that directors who win Academy Awards are few and far between. However, you can make a comfortable living if you have realistic career goals. Advance your career slowly, but keep it moving. Persistence, in the long run, always wins.

Many novice directors are convinced they must move to Los Angeles or New York in order to take their first step on the ladder to success. *Don't move!* In fact, don't give up your nine-to-five job.

Start your directing career in your hometown! Most likely, there are video companies in your city making television commercials for local merchants or taping such events as graduations, Bar/Bat Mitzvahs and weddings. Get to know these companies; see if they will let you get your feet wet by videotaping some of them. Later, try moving up to directing local commercials. Take these small jobs seriously. Utilize all you know about shooting on location, framing, lighting, staging and choreography. You'll be surprised at how much hands-on experience you'll gain.

How about directing a show at the local community theater. You will not only gain a deeper insight into how to make a written character come alive, but you will learn how to deal with actors and ways to get your ideas of character interpretation across.

Next, you should gain exposure by entering your work in film festivals. Most festivals accept dramatic shorts, documentaries, animation and full-length feature films. Most require a modest entrance fee. However, it is not easy to have a film accepted at one of the major festivals. Many of the larger festivals receive 40,000+ entries! So, look for the smaller festivals, which are more accepting of submissions. Hopefully, your work will be awarded a prize or gain some kind of positive acknowledgment. If it does neither, you'll still have satisfaction knowing that your film was accepted for exhibition. And, who knows? You could gain fame, be signed by an agent or have your film picked up for distribution. (A film does not necessarily have to win a prize to find a distributor. Many distributors sign films that screen out of the festival's competition.)

In a time when multi-million-dollar blockbusters and sequels dominate screens, festivals tend to cater to a more discriminating audience—viewers who appreciate artistic, independently-made films. Festivals now are filled with agents, acquisition executives for arthouse distributors and representatives from major studios—all looking for new talent. In fact, when a major festival announces its selections, films on the list suddenly will become "hot."

However, you should not feel obligated to deplete your financial resources by producing a feature-length film for submission to a festival. While some festivals (The Sundance Film Festival among them) only accept 35mm full-length projects, the majority of them (domestic and foreign) accept a variety of film types, lengths and formats, i.e., 35mm, 16mm, Super 8, and videotapes. To receive information on film festivals you should contact:

Association of Independent Video
and Filmmakers (AIVF)
625 Broadway
New York, NY 10012

Your local library may carry the latest *AIVF Guide to International Film and Video Festivals* (compiled by Kathryn Bowser). Festival addresses and rules change frequently, so the most recent issue is the best. You can also find information about film festivals on the web at http://www.filmfestivals.com.

Film festivals take place worldwide and include local exhibitions (Palm Springs Film Festival, Aspen Shortfest, Santa Barbara Film Festival, etc.), alternative distribution networks (Toronto International Film Festival, Sundance and high-powered film markets, such as Cannes Film Festival (France), MIFED (Italy), Berlin International Film Festival (Germany) and the American Film Market (USA).

If you want to try to the festival circuit, start by:

- Entering a short film or videotape. (A 15- to 20-minute production is fine.)
- Attend a film festival. (*See* what is being made; evaluate other filmmakers' entries and make yours better.)

Your film should not be ordinary or it will get lost in the mass-exhibited projects. *Your film must stand out*; it must be unique. Sound impossible? Perhaps. But, if you concentrate on your best and strongest directing abilities, it may not seem that impossible. For example, your talent may lie in developing relationships between characters; maybe you are stronger in staging and choreography; perhaps you excel in visualization symbolism via creative lighting and innovative camera movements. Be specific. Do things differently from other directors. Force the recognition you deserve.

Once you have directed a number of local television commercials and have exhibited and gained a measure of recognition at a number of film festivals, it is time to find representation. Don't be persuaded by phony agents or managers—those who promise too much, take your money *(agents are not paid up front)* and deliver nothing. Limit your search to franchised agencies only. You may obtain a list of franchised agents from:

Directors Guild of America West
7920 Sunset Boulevard
Los Angeles, CA 90046

Directors Guild of America
110 West 57th Street
New York, NY 10019

Directors Guild of America
520 North Michigan Avenue
Chicago, IL 60611

The Director's Guild of America also maintains a web site at http://www.dga.org.

8.2 The Interviews

You will encounter two different types of interviews: the *Directed Interview* (during which the interviewer asks you direct questions pertaining to your résumé, experience and demo reel); the *Non-Directed Interview* (which consists of informal, unrelated questions). If you participate in a Non-Directed Interview, the agent and/or producer has been sold on your talent; now he needs to find out what kind of person you are.

The way you present yourself to others reveals to them clues about you as a person and about your working habits.

Following are a few points to take into consideration:
- Dress neatly, not flashy;
- Do not wear distracting jewelry;
- Have your hair combed neatly;
- Avoid strong perfume or shaving lotion.

Expect stress before and during the interview. Counteract this tension by utilizing the *Positive Reaction* exercise below:
- Relax your body;
- Smile;
- Have confidence in yourself and in your abilities;
- Enter the agent's or producer's office with your chin up.
- Prepare questions YOU want to ask.
- Here are a few helpful tips:
- Verify the interview's time and place. If you're uncertain about location and directions, take a dry run to the office before the interview.
- Find out where you can park.
- Arrive ahead of your scheduled interview time.

- Know your interviewer's name. (Agencies often have many agents on staff.)
- Have on hand an extra copy of your résumé.
- When you first meet your interviewer, make eye contact with him and smile.
- Don't shake hands with your interviewer until he extends his hand first.
- Use his first name ONLY if he invites you to do so.
- Don't hesitate to ask the interviewer questions.
- If uncertain about a question, have it rephrased.
- Be honestly enthusiastic about the project.
- Be positive about your work and stress your accomplishments—without bragging.
- If unsure about how to respond, give yourself a moment to think.
- Don't say negative things or show a negative attitude.
- Don't criticize another agent and / or producer with whom you had previously interviewed.
- Throughout the interview, pay attention to body language (yours and the interviewer's), tone of voice and eye contact.

Immediately after your interview, jot down:
- Questions the interviewer asked;
- What aspects of the interview went well and what aspects didn't;
- Ways on improving your interview technique.

Whether or not you expect to be signed by the agent or offered a directing assignment, write your interviewer a thank you note, including:
- Your appreciation for having been granted an interview;

- Your certainty that you will be an asset to the agency's client list or to the production company's team.
- Your résumé's most important achievements;
- Your hope to be signed/and or considered for the assignment.

There are certain elements of your persona which will affect your interviews—positively or negatively.

<u>Your Body Language</u>. Present yourself as the winner you are—through *body language*, which tells others what you're like, what you think about yourself and how pleasant it will be to work with you. Strengthen that first good impression you gave as you entered the interviewer's office. Be sure to:

- Sit attentively, but in a relaxed manner.
- Show your attention and appreciation by nodding, making eye contact and shifting your head-and-shoulder positions while listening. (Watch TV talk-show hosts; they have refined the art of listening.)
- Look at your interviewer.
- Give your comments added importance by leaning slightly forward when it is your turn to speak.

And now, avoid the most common signs of insecurity. Never:

- Lean back—you'll remove yourself from the topic and the interviewer.
- Cross your arms in front of your chest; this is a classic defensive position that shows you feel threatened.
- Rub the back of your neck, showing your uneasiness.
- Rub or touch your nose, indicating that you are taking a dim view of your interviewer's comments.
- Cover your mouth with your hands while you speak, showing your uncertainty about your opinion or yourself.

- Jingle change or car keys in your pocket or fiddle with your jewelry, sure signs of your insecurity, fear and/or low self-esteem.

Making Eye Contact and Smiling. Nothing tells more about your self-confidence than the way you look at another. Therefore, regardless how nervous, afraid or hesitant you are, do not avoid your interviewer's eyes by looking down. Do combine your straightforward gaze with a friendly smile of self-confidence.

Your Voice. Many people wrongly equate voice quality with personality. Since it is difficult to gauge your own voice, tape record it and then ask yourself:

- Does my voice sound friendly?
- Does my voice sound authoritative?
- Do I speak distinctly?

Some people don't warm up to a subject right away, and until they do, they speak with a monotone delivery: everything they say, regardless how important or interesting, is kept on the same intensity level. Remember our discussion on the different communication levels employed by skilled actors (2.3, "Communication Levels")? The same holds true for interviews and negotiations. Vary your delivery between Intensity/Communication Level I (*"I want to explain"*) and Intensity/Communication Level II (*"I want to make a point"*). I would recommend staying away from Intensity/Communication Level III (*"I want to force"*).

GOALS

The goals you set and the steps you take to achieve those goals determines whether or not you will utilize your talent and experience to the fullest. Remember: goals cannot be achieved overnight. Therefore, always keep a clear picture of *what you want to achieve* and *how you will go about it*. Your first step is to break down your goals into several categories:

- Your Main Goal;
- Intermediate Goal (within one or two years);
- Short-range Goals (within three to six months).

At regular intervals, review your goals. Since your Main Goal is set (i.e., to direct quality films), you'll probably only need to jot down your Intermediate Goal and when you want to achieve it. Then, list your Short-Range Goals; list as many as possible. At your next personal review, eliminate the Short-Range Goals you have achieved and set new ones that eventually will bring you closer to your Intermediate Goal. At these regular reviews, modify your Short-Range Goals, change others, cancel some and create new ones. Since, at this point in your career, you have little control over your Main Goal, set as many Short-Range Goals as possible, selecting goals you can *control*. Accomplishing Short-Range Goals will get you used to success; it will make you expect success. It is this *expectation of success* that vastly increases your chances of controlling your Intermediate and Main Goals.

8.3 Information-Achievement Cycle

Whether or not you'll be able to utilize your assets to the fullest depends upon the information at your disposal. Information leads to achievement, which leads to new information, which leads to new achievement, etc.

The *Information-Achievement Cycle* will help you set your Short-Range Goals, which, eventually, will lead to success. For Example

- Understand that a wide range of information leads to the accomplishment of goals.
- Recognize specific obstacles that keep you from achieving your goals and learn ways to overcome and / or sidestep them.
- Know how to make effective decisions.

This ever-increasing spiral of information leading to achievement looks something like this:

Information
accumulating knowledge to set your goal
▼
Experience
using the acquired information
▼
Achievement
reaching your goal
▼
Information
accumulating new knowledge necessary to set new goals

Following is a Sample Information-Achievement Cycle that could be similar to one you might create for your goals.

MAIN GOAL
"I want to direct quality motion pictures."
Obstacle
"Without agency representation,
it is almost impossible to find a directing job."
▼

INTERMEDIATE GOAL
"Get signed by a franchised agency."
Obstacle
"Without extensive directing credits (exposure),
no agency will sign me."
▼

DECISION
"I need several short-range goals
which will help me receive needed exposure."
▼

SHORT-RANGE GOAL 1
"Win a prize at a film festival."
▼

INFORMATION
Obtain a list of film festivals.
Find out about topic and cost.
What is the preferred format: video or film?
What is the preferred length?
Ways to finance the project.
▼

ACHIEVEMENT
Shot my project.
Exhibit at several film festivals.
▼

SHORT-RANGE GOAL 2
Find work (and directing experience)
with a local video company.
▼

INFORMATION
Look through the Yellow Pages.
Check with friends and acquaintances—get leads.
Make calls and set up interviews.
▼

ACHIEVEMENT
Got a job.
▼

SHORT-RANGE GOAL 3:
Do some location work for a local TV station.
▼

INFORMATION
Call stations and find out whom to contact.
Send résumé (directing/taping work,
degree from film school, etc.)
to the appropriate contact.
After a week, call and inquire about an interview.
▼

ACHIEVEMENT
You received a job offer.
You accepted it, even though the job was
an entry-level position.
▼

SHORT RANGE GOAL 4
Direct local stage productions.
▼

INFORMATION
Find out who is in charge of the
local community theaters.
Call and explain you'd like to help cast
and/or direct a play.
Send in your résumé.
▼

ACHIEVEMENT
Accepted for an unpaid job.
Took it.
▼

SHORT RANGE GOAL 5
Direct acting students in front of the camera.
▼

INFORMATION
Find out whether the local university offers
Extension classes.
Contact Extension director.
Suggest a seminar or course on
"Actors in Front of the Camera."
Explain you can direct students' movements
in front of a camera,
such as Reversals, Two-Shots and Close Ups.
▼

ACHIEVEMENT
Offered a part-time teaching position.
Took it.

You won't reach all of your Short-Range Goals (that's why you'll always be updating your list and selecting new ones), but each goal you do reach will bring you closer to your Intermediate Goal—to be signed by a franchised agent. Once signed, you may be offered Assistant Director (AD) jobs, and perhaps a small directing assignment. Each assignment should move you closer to your Main Goal.

After a couple of years, you might want to produce a movie of your own. When this happens, you'll again apply the Information-Achievement Cycle to your goals. But, this time, your goals will be different:
- Find the right script;
- Interest a star in your project;

- Obtain a *Letter of Intent* from a reliable distribution company;
- Arrange financing (i.e., through a law firm specializing in motion picture financing; through a consortium of investors, etc.).

Granted, producing a motion picture is not easy. You will have a long and arduous road ahead before you see your own feature film on the screen. But, it will be worth every step!

8.4 Decisions

Before you begin your career, you must know *what you want*, not what you *think you want* or what you *believe you should want*. Decisions always spell change and they often propel you in different directions. This is not as easy as it sounds! A common mistake people make when dealing with their problems is their tendency to "mull things over." Caught in this cycle, one reviews the same obstacles over again. Don't waste your time and energy! Look at your obstacle/problem from an objective perspective (from the outside):

- Define the obstacle/problem in one short sentence.
- Get rid of any pre-conceived ideas concerning the obstacle/problem.
- Gather correct and complete information.
- Draw your assumptions from the acquired information.
- Don't hesitate to give any unfamiliar or unorthodox assumption more thought.
- Ask yourself if you could possibly: (1) add elements; (2) combine elements; (3) eliminate elements; (4) rearrange elements.
- Arrive at sensible Pros and Cons.
- Make your decision.

Example

Decision
"Should I try to get signed by an agent now?"
Pros:
- Without agency representation, I won't get directing jobs.
- I am tired of the small directing jobs I currently have.
- I have saved enough money to move to Hollywood

and sustain myself for a while.

Cons:

- My demo reel and résumé are a bit weak.
- I might be signed by a mediocre agency.

Decision

- I won't move at this time.
- I'll produce a great short film that illustrates my directing abilities.
- I'll exhibit my short at film festivals. Hopefully, I'll win a prize.
- After I have a more effective demo reel, I'll contact agents.

CONCLUSION

Persistence counts! Determination will win out in the end! Success will be yours as long as you keep:

- Moving;
- Taking risks;
- Learning from your mistakes;
- Correcting your course whenever necessary;
- Making mature decisions.

And, most importantly, *you must keep believing in yourself.* Insist upon your rights. Do not let anyone belittle you or your goals. With these thoughts in mind, you'll build upon your successes.

Allow me to close this book with one of my grandmother's wise adages: "Life is not easy. You have to take life as it happens but you must try to make it happen the way you wish to take it."

Good luck and success to all of you.

God bless you.

APPENDIX A

Unions and Guilds

DIRECTORS

*Source: Film Directors: A Complete Guide
(Lone Eagle Publishing Co., 1997)*

USA

DIRECTORS GUILD OF AMERICA

West

7920 Sunset Blvd.
Los Angeles, CA 90046
310-289-2000
Fax: 213-289-3671
213-851-3671: Agency Information

East

110 West 57th Street
New York, NY 10019
212-581-0370
Fax: 212-581-1441

Midwest

400 North Michigan Avenue, Suite 307
Chicago, IL 60611
312-644-5050
Fax: 312-644-5776

AUSTRALIA

THE AUSTRALIAN SCREEN
DIRECTORS ASSOCIATION
P.O. Box 211
Rozelle 2039
Sydney, Australia
2-555-7045
2-810-2272
Fax: 2-555-7086

GREAT BRITAIN (UK)

DIRECTORS GUILD OF GREAT
BRITAIN
15-19 Great Titchfield Street
London W1P 7FB
171-436-8626
Fax: 171-436-8646

CANADA

DIRECTORS GUILD OF CANADA

National Office

387 Bloor Street East, Suite 401
Toronto, Ontario
M4W 1H7 Canada
416-972-0098
Fax: 416-972-6058

Alberta District Coucil

2219 – 2nd Street S.W.
Calgery, Alberta
T2S 1S8 Canada
403-244-3456
Fax: 403-245-5779

British Columbia District Council

1152 Mainland Street, Suite 430
Vancouver, British Columbia
V8B 2X4 Canada
604-688-2976
Fax: 604-688-2610

Nova Scotia District Council

1541 Barrington Street,
Suite 402
Halifax, Nova Scotia
B3J 1Z5 Canada
902-492-3424
Fax: 902-492-2678

Ontario District Council
225 Richmond Street West,
Suite 300
Toronto, Ontario
M5V 1W2 Canada
416-351-8200
Fax: 416-351-8205

Quebec District Council
4067 St. Lawrence Blvd.,
Suite 200
Montreal, Quebec
H2W 1Y7 Canada
514-844-4084
Fax: 514-844-1067

SCREEN ACTORS GUILD DIRECTORY OF OFFICES

Source: Screen Actors Guild
Note: A list of SAG-franchised agents is
available from SAG for a modest fee. This
list, plus other useful information from SAG,
is also available online at SAG's web site.
Their URL is: http//:www.sag.com.

NATIONAL OFFICE

HOLLYWOOD BRANCH

5757 Wilshire Blvd.
Los Angeles, CA 90036-3600
Main Switchboard: 213-954-1600
FAX: 213-549-6603
National Executive Director: Ken Orsatti
Hollywood Branch Executive Director:
Leonard Chassman

DEPARTMENTS:

Agency / Actors to Locate
  213-549-6737
Affirmative Action
  213-549-6644
Committee Office
  213-549-6418
Film Society
  213-549-6658
Theatrical Contracts
  213-549-6828
Television Contracts
  213-549-6842
Commercial Contracts
  213-549-6858

Industrial/Interactive Contracts
  213-549-6850
Membership/Dues
  213-549-6755
New Membership
  213-549-6769
Residuals
  213-549-6505
Signatory Information
  213-549-6869
Singers Rep
  213-549-6864
SAG Awards
  213-549-6707
SAFETY HOTLINE (24 hours)
  213-954-1600

NEW YORK

1515 Broadway, 44th Floor
New York, NY 10036
Main Switchboard 212-944-1030
FAX: 212-944-6774

DEPARTMENTS:

Agency
212-944-6797
Membership/Dues
212-944-6243
Signatory Info Line
212-827-1470
SAFETY HOTLINE (24 hours)
212-517-0909

BRANCH OFFICES:

ARIZONA

1616 E. Indian School Road,
Suite 330
Phoenix, AZ 85016
602-265-2712
FAX: 602-264-7571
Executive Director: Don Livesay

BOSTON

11 Beacon Street, Room 515
Boston, MA 02108
617-742-2688
FAX: 617-742-4904
Executive Director: Donna Sommers

CHICAGO
1 East Erie, Suite #650
Chicago, IL 60611
312-573-8081
Executive Director: Eileen Willenborg

CLEVELAND**
1030 Euclid Avenue, Suite #429
Cleveland, OH 44115
216-579-9305
FAX: 216-781-2257
Executive Director: Stephen Hatch
FAX: 312-573-0318
** Cleveland is an AFTRA Office which
also handles SAG business for area.

DENVER*
950 South Cherry Street, Suite 502
Denver, CO 80222
800-527-7517 or 303-757-6226
FAX: 303-757-1769
Executive Director: Jerre Hookey
*Denver is a regional office which also covers
New Mexico & Utah*

DALLAS
6060 N. Central Expressway
Suite 302, LB 604
214-363-8300
FAX: 214-363-5386
Executive Director: Ken Freehill

DETROIT
27770 Franklin Road
Southfield, MI 48034-2352
Phone: 248-355-3105
FAX: 248-355-2879
Executive Director: Barbara
Honner

FLORIDA*
7300 North Kendall Drive, Suite #620
Miami, FL 33156-7840
305-670-7677
FAX: 305-670-1813
Executive Director: Mel Karl
*Florida is a regional office which also
covers Alabama, Arkansas, Louisiana,
Mississippi, No. Carolina, So. Carolina,
West Virginia, U.S.Virgin Islands, Puerto
Rico & the Caribbean*

FLORIDA (CENTRAL)
646 West Colonial Drive
Orlando, FL 32804-7342
407-649-3100
407-649-7222
Executive Director: Joel Binford

GEORGIA
455 E. Paces Ferry Road NE, Suite 334
Atlanta, GA 30305
404-239-0131
FAX: 404-239-0137
Executive Director: Melissa Goodman

HAWAII
949 Kapiolani Blvd., #105
Honolulu, HI 96814
808-538-0388
FAX: 808-593-2636
Executive Director: Brenda Ching

HOUSTON
2650 Fountainview, #326
Houston, TX 77057
713-972-1806
FAX: 713-780-0261
Executive Director: Jack Dunlop

LAS VEGAS
3900 Paradise Road, Suite #206
Las Vegas, NV 89109
702-737-8818
FAX: 702-737-8851
Executive Director: Bobbi Hughes

MINNEAPOLIS / ST.PAUL
708 North 1st Street, Suite #333
Minneapolis, MN 55401
612-371-9120
FAX: 612-371-9119
Executive Director: Colleen Aho

NASHVILLE
P.O. Box 121087
Nashville, TN 37212
615-327-2944
FAX: 615-329-2803
Executive Director: Randall Himes

NORTH CAROLINA
321 North Front Street
Wilmington, NC 28401
910-762-1889
FAX: 910-762-0881
Executive Director: Julie Balter

OREGON
3030 S.W. Moody, Suite #104
Portland, OR 97201
503-279-9600
FAX: 503-279-9603
Executive Director: Stuart
Pemble-Belkin

PHILADELPHIA
230 South Broad Street, 10th floor
Philadelphia, PA 19102
215-545-3150
FAX: 215-732-0086
Executive Director: John Kailin

ST. LOUIS**
1310 Papin Street, Suite #103
St. Louis, MO 63103
314-231-8410
FAX: 314-231-8412
Executive Director: Jackie Dietrich
FAX 619-278-2505
*** St. Louis is an AFTRA Office which also
handles SAG business for this area.*

SAN DIEGO
7827 Convoy Court, Suite #400
San Diego, CA 92111
619-278-7695
Executive Director: Tom Doyle

SAN FRANCISCO
235 Pine Street, 11th floor
San Francisco, CA 94104
415-391-7510
FAX 415-391-1108
Executive Director: Rebecca Rhine

SEATTLE
601 Valley Street, Suite #100
Seattle, WA 98109
206-270-0493
FAX: 206-282-7073
Executive Director: Joan Kalhorn

WASHINGTON, D.C. / BALTIMORE
4340 East W. Highway, Suite #204
Bethesda, MD 20814
301-657-2560
FAX 301-656-3615
Executive Director: Patricia O'Donnell

WRITERS

<u>USA</u>

WRITERS GUILD OF AMERICA
West
7000 West Third Street
Los Angeles, CA 90048-4329
213-951-4000
213-782-4502 (Agency Information)

Esst
555 West 57th Street
New York, NY 10019
212-245-6180

<u>GREAT BRITAIN</u>

WRITERS GUILD OF GREAT BRITAIN
430 Edgeware Road
London W21 EH
England
171-723-8074

OTHER CRAFTSPEOPLE

AMERICAN SOCIETY
OF CINEMATOGRAPHERS (ASC)
PO Box 2230
Hollywood, CA 90078

<u>CAMERAPERSONS</u>

IATSE LOCAL 644
Louis D'Agostino
80 8th Ave
New York, NY 10018
212-647-7300

IATSE Local 659
Lorna Wiley, Secretary
7714 Sunset Blvd.
Suite 300
Hollywood, CA 91423
213-876-0160

COSTUME DESIGNERS

IATSE Local 892

Barbara Inglehart, Secretary
13949 Ventura Blvd.
Suite 309
Sherman Oaks, CA 91423
818-905-1557

MOTION PICTURE COSTUMERS

IATSE Local 705

Sandra Burke Jordan
1527 N. La Brea
Hollywood, CA 90028
213-851-0220

MOTION PICTURE EDITORS

IATSE Local 776 (Los Angeles)

Ron Kutak, Business Agent
7715 Sunset Blvd., Suite 200
Hollywood, CA 90046
213-876-4770

IATSE Local 771 (New York)

William Hanauer, Business Agent
165 W. 49th St., Suite900
New York, NY 10036
212-302-0771

MOTION PICTURE SET PAINTERS

IATSE Local 729

Carmine Palazzo, Business Agent
11365 Ventura Blvd., Suite 202
Studio City, CA 91604
818-984-3000

SOCIETY OF MOTION PICTURE AND TELEVISION ART DIRECTORS

IATSE Local 876

Gene Allen, Executive Director
11365 Ventura Blvd., Suite 315
Studio City, CA 91604
818-762-9995

SOCIETY OF MOTION PICTURE AND TELEVISION ENGINEERS (SMPTE)

595 W Hartsdale Ave.
White Plains, NY 10607-1824

THE SOCIETY OF OPERATING CAMERAMEN (SOC)

PO Box 2006
Toluca Lake, CA 91610
818-382-7070

APPENDIX B

International Film Commissions

Source: AFCI

AIR NIUGINI
P.O. Box 7186
Boroko, Papua New Guinea
PAPUA NEW GUINEA
675-3-273-415
FAX: 675-3-273-380

ALABAMA FILM OFFICE
401 Adams Avenue
Montgomery, AL 36130 USA
800-633-5898
FAX: 334-242-2077

ALASKA FILM OFFICE
3601 C Street, Suite 700
Anchorage, AK 99503 USA
907-269-8137
FAX: 907-269-8136

ALBERTA FILM COMMISSION
6th Floor, 639 - 5 Ave. SW
The Standard Life Tower
PO Box 2100, Station (M)
Calgary, AB T2P 2M5 Canada
403-221-7826
FAX: 403-221-7837

ALBUQUERQUE TV & FILM OFFICE
20 First Plaza NW, Suite 601
Albuquerque, NM 87102 USA
505-842-9918
800-733-9918
FAX: 505-247-9101

AMARILLO FILM OFFICE
1000 South Polk Street
Amarillo, TX 79101 USA
806-374-1497
800-692-1338
FAX: 806-373-3909

APACHE JUNCTION CHAMBER
OF COMMERCE
PO Box 1747
Apache Junction, AZ 85217-1747 USA
602-982-3141
FAX: 602-982-3234

ARIZONA FILM COMMISSION
3800 North Central, Building D
Phoenix, AZ 85012 USA
602-280-1380
800-523-6695
FAX: 602-280-1384

ARKANSAS MOTION PICTURE OFFICE
1 State Capital Mall, Room 2C-200
Little Rock, AR 72201 USA
501-682-7676
FAX: 501-682-FILM

AUSTIN FILM OFFICE
201 E. Second Street
Austin, TX 78701 USA
512-404-4562
800-926-2282 x-4562
FAX: 512-404-4564

BAHAMAS FILM AND TELEVISION
COMMISSION
3450 Wilshire Boulevard, Suite 208
Los Angeles, CA 90010 USA
213-385-0033
FAX: 213-383-3966

BATH FILM OFFICE
The Pump Room, Stall Street
Bath, Avon BA1 1LZ
UNITED KINGDOM
44-1225-477-711
FAX: 44-1225-477-221

BERKELEY CVB/BERKELEY FILM
OFFICE
1834 University Avenue, 1st Floor
Berkeley, CA 94703 USA
510-549-7040
800-847-4823
FAX: 510-644-2052

BIG BEAR LAKE FILM OFFICE
39707 Big Bear Boulevard
PO Box 10000
Big Bear Lake, CA 92315 USA
909-878-3040
FAX: 909-866-6766

BIG ISLAND FILM OFFICE
25 Aupuni Street, Room 219
Hilo, HI 96720 USA
808-961-8366
FAX: 808-935-1205

BORDEAUX FILM COMMISSION
12 Place de la Bourse
Bordeaux, 33076 FRANCE
33-56-79 50 14
FAX: 33-56-79 52 67

BOULDER COUNTY FILM
COMMISSION
PO Box 73
Boulder, CO 80306 USA
303-442-1044
800-444-0447
FAX: 303-938-8837

BRITISH COLUMBIA FILM
COMMISSION
601 West Cordova Street
Vancouver, BC V6B 1G1 CANADA
604-660-2732
FAX: 604-660-4790

BRITISH FILM COMMISSION
70 Baker Street
London, W1M 1DJ ENGLAND
44-171-224-5000
info@bfc.co.uk
FAX: 44-171-224-1013

BUREAU DE CINEMA DO CEARA
Avenida Barao De Studart - 505
Fortaleza, BR - Ceara 60120-000 BRAZIL
55-85-244-4549
55-85-268-3199
FAX: 55-85-261-4733

CALGARY FILM OFFICE
PO Box 2100, Station M (#6)
Calgary, AB T2P 2M5 CANADA
403-221-7826
FAX: 403-221-7837

CALIFORNIA FILM COMMISSION
6922 Hollywood Boulevard, Suite 600
Hollywood, CA 90028-6126 USA
213-736-2465
800-858-4PIX
FilmCA@aol.com
FAX: 213-736-2522

CANARIVISION – CANARY ISLANDS
FILM COMM.
s/n.Edif.Sovhispan, of.206, S C de Tenerife
38004 SPAIN
34-22-240038
34-22-240057
FAX: 34-22-240060

CARDIFF FILM COMMISSION
The Media Centre, Culverhouse Cross
Cardiff, Wales CF5 6XJ
UNITED KINGDOM
44-1222-590-240
FAX: 44-1222-590-511

CATALINA ISLAND FILM
COMMISSION
PO Box 217
Avalon, CA 90704 USA
310-510-7646
FAX: 310-510-1646

CEDAR RAPIDS AREA FILM
COMMISSION
119 First Avenue SE
PO Box 5339
Cedar Rapids, IA 52406-5339 USA
319-398-5009 x-27
800-735-5557 x-27
FAX: 319-398-5089

CENTRAL ENGLAND SCREEN
COMMISSION
Waterside House, 46 Gas Street
Birmingham, ENGLAND B1 2JT UNITED
KINGDOM
44-121-643-9309
FAX: 44-121-643-9064
Nottingham Office: 44-115-952-7870
FAX:
44-115-952-0539
E-mail: emdcwelcome@attmail.com
Web: http://www.emnet.co.uk/clients/e/
emscreen-Commission/

CENTRAL FLORIDA DEVELOPMENT
COUNCIL, INC.
600 North Broadway, #300
Bartow, FL 33830 USA
941-534-4370
FAX: 941-533-1247

CENTRAL UTAH FILM COMMISSION
51 South University Avenue, Suite 110
P. O. Box 912
Provo, UT 84601 USA
801-370-8390
800-222-8824
Utah
County.UCHLTH.Marilyn@Email.state.ut.us
FAX: 801-370-8050

CHARLOTTE REGION FILM OFFICE
112 S. Tryon Street, Suite 900
Charlotte, NC 28284 USA
800-554-4373
704-347-8942
FAX: 704-347-8981

CHEYENNE AREA FILM OFFICE
309 W. Lincolnway
Cheyenne, WY 82001 USA
307-778-3133
1-800-426-5009
FAX: 307-778-3190

CHICAGO FILM OFFICE
1 North LaSalle, Suite 2165
Chicago, IL 60602 USA
312-744-6415
FAX: 312-744-1378

CHICO CHAMBER/BUTTE COUNTY
FILM COMMISSION
500 Main Street
PO Box 3038
Chico, CA 95927 USA
916-891-5556 x 326
800-852-8570
FAX: 916-891-3613

CINEAUSTRIA
11601 Wilshire Boulevard, Suite 2480
Los Angeles, CA 90025 USA
310-477-2038
FAX: 310-477-5141

CITY OF FILLMORE FILM
COMMISSION
524 Sespe Ave.
P.O. Box 487
Fillmore, CA 93016 USA
805-524-3701
FAX: 805-524-5707

CITY OF PASADENA
100 North Garfield Avenue, #103
Pasadena, CA 91109 USA
818-405-4152
FAX: 818-405-4785

CITY OF PHOENIX FILM OFFICE
200 West Washington, 10th Floor
Phoenix, AZ 85003-1611 USA
602-262-4850
FAX: 602-534-2295

CITY OF PRESCOTT
P.O. Box 2059
Prescott, AZ 86302 USA
520-445-3500
FAX: 520-776-6255

CITY OF REGINA
P.O. BOX 1790
Regina, SASK S4P 3C8 CANADA
306-777-7486
FAX: 306-777-6803

CITY OF WEST HOLLYWOOD
8300 Santa Monica Boulevard
West Hollywood, CA 90069-4314 USA
213-848-6489
FAX: 310-289-9541

COCHISE COUNTY FILM COMMISSION
1415 W. Melody Lane, Building B
Bisbee, AZ 85603 USA
520-432-9454
520-432-9200
FAX: 520-432-5016

COLORADO MOTION PICTURE & TV
COMMISSION
1625 Broadway, Suite #1700
Denver, CO 80202 USA
303-620-4500
FAX: 303-620-4545

COLORADO SPRINGS FILM
COMMISSION
6 North Tejon, Suite 400
P. O. Box 1575
Colorado Springs, CO 80903 USA
719-578-6943
FAX: 719-578-6394

COLUMBUS FILM COMMISSION
P.O. Box 789
Columbus, MS 39703 USA
601-329-1191
800-327-2686
FAX: 601-329-8969

COMMISSION NATIONALE DU FILM
FRANCE
30, avenue de Messine
Paris, 75008 FRANCE
33-1-53-83-9898
FAX: 33-1-53-83-9899

CONNECTICUT FILM, VIDEO & MEDIA
OFFICE
865 Brook Street
Rocky Hill, CT 06067-3405 USA
203-258-4339
203-258-4399
203-258-4301
FAX: 203-258-4275

DALLAS/FORT WORTH REGIONAL
FILM COMM.
P.O. Box 610246
DFW Airport, TX 75261 USA
214-621-0400
800-234-5699
FAX: 214-929-0916

DANBURY FILM OFFICE
46 Main Street (06810)
P.O. Box 406
Danbury, CT 6813 USA
203-743-0546
800-841-4488
FAX: 203-790-6124

DELAWARE FILM OFFICE
99 Kings Highway
P.O. Box 1401
Dover, DE 19903 USA
302-739-4271
800-441-8846
FAX: 302-739-5749

DURHAM CONVENTION & VISITORS
BUREAU
101 East Morgan Street
Durham, NC 27701 USA
919-680-8314
800-446-8604
FAX: 919-683-9555

EASTERN SCREEN
Anglia Television - Royal Hotel
Norwich, Norfolk, U.K. NR1 3JG
ENGLAND
+44-1603-767 077
FAX: +44-1603-767 191

EDINBURGH & LOTHIAN SCREEN
INDUSTRIES
Filmhouse, 88 Lothian Road
Edinburgh, EH3 9BZ SCOTLAND
44-131-228-5960
FAX: 44-131-228-5967

EDMONTON MOTION PICTURE & TV
BUREAU
9797 Jasper Avenue NW
Edmonton, AB T5J 1N9 CANADA
403-424-9191
800-661-6965
FAX: 403-426-0236

EL DORADO/TAHOE FILM
COMMISSION
542 Main Street
Placerville, CA 95667 USA
916-626-4400
800-457-6279
FAX: 916-642-1624

EL PASO FILM COMMISSION
1 Civic Center Plaza
El Paso, TX 79901 USA
915-534-0698
800-351-6024
FAX: 915-534-0686

ENTERTAINMENT INDUSTRY
DEVELOPMENT CORP.
6922 Hollywood Boulevard, Suite #606
Los Angeles, CA 90028 USA
213-957-1000 x3
FAX: 213-463-0613

EUREKA-HUMBOLDT COUNTY CVB
1034 Second Street
Eureka, CA 95501-0541 USA
707-443-5097
800-346-3482
FAX: 707-443-5115

FILM & TELEVISION OFFICE
200 East Las Olas Boulevard, Ste #1850
Fort Lauderdale, FL 33301 USA
305-524-3113
800-741-1420
FAX: 305-524-3167

FILM NEW BRUNSWICK
P.O. Box 6000
Fredericton, NB E3B 5H1 CANADA
506-453-2553
FAX: 506-453-2416

FILM NEW ZEALAND
P. O. Box 24-142
Wellington, North Island NEW ZEALAND
64-4-801 5794
FAX: 64-4-384-9710

FLAGSTAFF FILM COMMISSION
405 N. Beaver Street, Building A, Suite 3
FlagStaff, AZ 86001 USA
520-779-7658
FAX: 520-556-0940

FLORIDA ENTERTAINMENT
COMMISSION
505 17th Street
Miami Beach, FL 33139 USA
305-673-7468
FAX: 305-673-7168

FLORIDA KEYS & KEY WEST FILM
COMMISSION
402 Wall Street
P.O. Box 984
Key West, FL 33040 USA
305-294-5988
800-527-8539
800-Film Keys
FAX: 305-294-7806

FORT MORGAN AREA FILM
COMMISSION
710 East Railroad Avenue
P.O. Box 100
Fort Morgan, CO 80701 USA
970-867-4310
FAX: 970-867-3039

FRESNO CONVENTION & VISITORS
BUREAU
808 M Street
Fresno, CA 93721 USA
800-788-0836
209-233-0836
FAX: 209-445-0122

GEORGIA FILM & VIDEOTAPE OFFICE
285 Peachtree Center Ave., Ste 1000
Atlanta, GA 30303 USA
404-656-3591
FAX: 404-651-9063

GHANA FILM COMMISSION
8306 Wilshire Boulevard, #330
Beverly Hills, CA 90211 USA
213-464-8343
FAX: 213-852-4926

GLOBE FILM COMMISSION
1360 North Broad Street, U.S. 60
P.O. Box 2539
Globe, AZ 85502 USA
520-425-4495
800-804-5623
FAX: 520-425-3410

GREATER CINCINNATI FILM
COMMISSION
632 Vine Street, #1010
Cincinnati, OH 45202 USA
513-784-1744
FAX: 513-768-8963

GREATER PHILADELPHIA FILM
OFFICE
1600 Arch Street, 12th Floor
Philadelphia, PA 19103 USA
215-686-2668
sharon@film.org
FAX: 215-686-3659

GREELEY/WELD COUNTY FILM
COMMISSION
1407 8th Avenue
Greeley, CO 80631 USA
970-352-3566
FAX: 970-352-3572

GREENWOOD CONVENTION &
VISITORS BUREAU
P. O. Drawer 739
Greenwood, MS 38935-0739 USA
601-453-9197
800-748-9064
FAX: 601-453-5526

GWYNEDD FILM OFFICE/MARKETING
& TOURISM
Gwynedd County Council 2
Bangor, Gwynedd LL57 4BN WALES
44-1248-670007
FAX: 44-1248-670112

HAWAII FILM OFFICE
P.O. Box 2359
Honolulu, HI 96804 USA
808-586-2570
FAX: 808-586-2572

HOLBROOK FILM COMMISSION
465 North First Avenue
P.O. Box 70
Holbrook, AZ 86025 USA
520-524-6225
FAX: 520-524-2159

HONG KONG TOURIST ASSOCIATION
10940 Wilshire Boulevard, Suite 1220
Los Angeles, CA 90024 USA
310-208-2678
FAX: 310-208-1869

HOUSTON FILM COMMISSION
801 Congress
Houston, TX 77002 USA
713-227-3100
800-365-7575
FAX: 713-223-3816

HUDSON VALLEY FILM & VIDEO
OFFICE, INC.
40 Garden Street, 2nd Floor
Poughkeepsie, NY 12601 USA
914-473-0318
FAX: 914-473-0082

IDAHO FILM BUREAU
700 West State Street, Box 83720
Boise, ID 83720-0093 USA
208-334-2470
800-942-8338
FAX: 208-334-2631

ILLINOIS FILM OFFICE
100 West Randolph, Suite 3-400
Chicago, IL 60601 USA
312-814-3600
FAX: 312-814-8874

IMPERIAL COUNTY FILM
COMMISSION
940 West Main Street, Suite 208
El Centro, CA 92243 USA
619-339-4290
800-345-6437
FAX: 619-352-7876

INDIANA FILM COMMISSION
1 North Capitol, #700
Indianapolis, IN 46204-2288 USA
317-232-8829
FAX: 317-233-6887

IOWA FILM OFFICE
200 East Grand Avenue
Des Moines, IA 50309 USA
515-242-4726
FAX: 515-242-4859

IRVING TEXAS FILM COMMISSION
6309 North O'Connor Road, Suite 222
Irving, TX 75039-3500 USA
214-869-0303
800-2-IRVING
FAX: 214-869-4609

ISLE OF MAN FILM COMMISSION
Sea Terminal Buildings
Douglas, Isle of Man IM1 2RG Great
Britain
44-1624-686846
FAX: 44-1624-686800

JAMPRO/JAMAICA FILM, MUSIC &
ENT. COMM.
35 Trafalgar Road, 3rd Floor
Kingston, W.I. 10 JAMAICA
809-929-9450
809-926-4613
FAX: 809-924-9650

JACKSONVILLE FILM & TV OFFICE
128 East Forsythe Street, Suite 505
Jacksonville, FL 32202 USA
904-630-2522
904-630-1622
FAX: 904-630-1485

STAFF: HEATHER SURFACE, PUBLIC
RELATIONS/FILM & VIDEO
SPECIALIST

JEFF DAVIS PARISH FILM
COMMISSION
P.O. Box 1207
Jennings, LA 70546-1207 USA
318-821-5534
FAX: 318-821-5536

KANAB/KANE COUNTY FILM
COMMISSION
78 S 100 E
Kanab, UT 84741 USA
801-644-5033
800-SEE-KANE
FAX: 801-644-5923

KANSAS CITY, MISSOURI FILM
OFFICE
10 Petticoat Lane, Suite 250
Kansas City, MO 64106 USA
816-221-0636
800-889-0636
FAX: 816-221-0189

KANSAS FILM COMMISSION
700 SW Harrison Street, Suite 1300
Topeka, KS 66603 USA
913-296-4927
FAX: 913-296-6988

KANSAS III FILM COMMISSION/
LAWRENCE CVB
734 Vermont
Lawrence, KS 66044 USA
913-865-4411
FAX: 913-865-4400

KAUAI FILM COMMISSION
4280-B Rice Street
Lihue, HI 96766 USA
808-241-6390
FAX: 808-241-6399

KENTUCKY FILM COMMISSION
500 Mero Street, 2200 Capitol Plz Tower
Frankfort, KY 40601 USA
502-564-3456
800-345-6591
FAX: 502-564-7588

KERN COUNTY BOARD OF TRADE
2101 Oak Street
P. O. Bin 1312
Bakersfield, CA 93302 USA
805-861-2367
800-500-KERN
FAX: 805-861-2017

LAS CRUCES FILM COMMISSION
311 North Downtown Mall
Las Cruces, NM 88001 USA
505-524-8521
800-FIESTAS
505-525-2112 (prvt)
FAX: 505-524-8191

LONDON FILM COMMISSION
12 Raddington Road - Ladbroke Grove
London, ENGLAND W105TG
UNITED KINGDOM
44-181-968-0968
FAX: 44-181-968-0177

LONG BEACH OFFICE
OF SPECIAL EVENTS
333 W. Ocean Blvd., 13th Floor
Long Beach, CA 90802 USA
310-570-5333
FAX: 310-570-5335

LOS ALAMOS COUNTY FILM
COMMISSION
P.O. Box 460
Los Alamos, NM 87544-0460 USA
505-662-8401
FAX: 505-662-8399

LOUISIANA FILM COMMISSION
P.O. Box 44320
Baton Rouge, LA 70804-4320 USA
504-342-8150
FAX: 504-342-7988

MALIBU CITY FILM COMMISSION
23555 Civic Center Way
Malibu, CA 91360 USA
310-456-2489 x-236
FAX: 310-456-5799

MAMMOTH LOCATION SERVICES
1 Minaret Road
P. O. Box 24
Mammoth Lakes, CA 93546 USA
619-934-0628
800-228-4947
FAX: 619-934-0700

MANCHESTER FILM OFFICE
Churchgate House - 56 Oxford Road
Manchester, ENGLAND M1 6EU UNITED
KINGDOM
44-161-237-1010
FAX: 44-161-228-2964

MANHATTAN FILM COMMISSION
555 Poyntz, Suite 290
Manhattan, KS 66502 USA
913-776-8829
800-759-0134

MANITOBA FILM & SOUND
DEVELOPMENT CORP.
Suite 333-93 Lombard Avenue
Winnipeg, MB R3B 3B1 CANADA
204-947-2040
explore@mbfilmsound.mb.ca
FAX: 204-956-5261

MARYLAND FILM OFFICE
217 E. Redwood Street, 9th Floor
Baltimore, MD 21202 USA
410-767-6340
800-333-6632
410-767-0067
FAX: 410-333-0044

MASSACHUSETTS FILM OFFICE
10 Park Plaza, Suite 2310
Boston, MA 2116 USA
617-973-8800
FAX: 617-973-8810

MAYOR'S OFFICE OF ART, CULTURE &
FILM
280 14th Street
Denver, CO 80202 USA
303-640-2686
FAX: 303-640-2737

MELBOURNE FILM OFFICE
Level 4, 49 Spring Street
Melbourne, Victoria 3000 AUSTRALIA
61-3-9651-0610
FAX: 61-3-9651-0606

MEMPHIS & SHELBY CTY FILM, TAPE
& MUSIC
Beale Street Landing/245 Wagner Pl. #4
Memphis, TN 38103-3815 USA
901-527-8300
FAX: 901-527-8326

METRO ORLANDO FILM &
TELEVISION OFFICE
200 East Robinson Street, Suite #600
Orlando, FL 32801 USA
407-422-7159
FAX: 407-843-9514

METRO RICHMOND CVB & FILM
OFFICE
550 East Marshall Street
Richmond, VA 23219 USA
804-782-2777
800-370-9004
FAX: 804-780-2577

MEXICO CITY FILM COMMISSION
Atletas 2 Edif.De Camerinos Pasillo 'A'-201
Col.CC
Mexico City, C.P. 4220 MEXICO
525-689-1944
525-549-3060
FAX: 525-549-1418

MIAMI/DADE OFFICE OF FILM, TV, &
PRINT
111 Northwest 1st Street, Suite 2510
Miami, FL 33128 USA
305-375-3288
FAX: 305-375-3266
Coordinator; Sabrina Riley, Secretary

MICHIGAN FILM OFFICE
201 N. Washington Square, Victor Centre
5th Floor
Lansing, MI 48913 USA
517-373-0638
800-477-3456
FAX: 517-241-0593

MINNEAPOLIS OFF. OF FILM/VIDEO/
RECORDING
323M City Hall - 350 S. 5th Street
Minneapolis, MN 55415 USA
612-673-2947
Pager: 612-818-1221
FAX: 612-673-2011

MINNESOTA FILM BOARD
401 North 3rd Street, Suite 460
Minneapolis, MN 55401 USA
612-332-6493
info@mnfilm.org
FAX: 612-332-3735

MISSISSIPPI FILM OFFICE
Box 849
Jackson, MS 39205 USA
601-359-3297
wemling%gw@decd.state.ms.us.
FAX: 601-359-5757

MISSOURI FILM OFFICE
301 West High, Room 770
P.O. Box 118
Jefferson City, MO 65102 USA
573-751-9050
FAX: 573-751-7385

MOAB TO MONUMENT VALLEY FILM
COMMISSION
50 East Center #1
Moab, UT 84532 USA
801-259-6388
801-587-3235
FAX: 801-259-6399

MOBILE FILM OFFICE
150 South Royal Street
Mobile, AL 36602 USA
334-434-7304
FAX: 334-434-7659

MONTANA FILM OFFICE
1424 9th Avenue
Helena, MT 59620 USA
406-444-3762
800-553-4563
montanafilm@travel.mt.gov
FAX: 406-444-4191

MONTEREY COUNTY FILM
COMMISSION
801 Lighthouse Avenue
P.O. Box 111
Monterey, CA 93942-0111 USA
408-646-0910
FAX: 408-655-9244

MONTREAL FILM & TELEVISION
COMMMISSION
413 Saint-Jacques Street, 4th Floor
Montreal, QUE H2Y 1N9 CANADA
514-872-2883
FAX: 514-872-3409
Permits Coordinator

MOTION PICTURE DIVISION/C.E.D.
555 East Washington, Suite 5400
Las Vegas, NV 89101 USA
702-486-2711
FAX: 702-486-2712

MUNICH FILM INFORMATION OFFICE
Kaiserstrasse 39
Muenchen, D-80801 GERMANY
49-89-38 19 04-32
49-89-38 19 04-0
FAX: 49-89-38 19 04-38

NYC MAYOR'S OFF. OF FILM/
THEATRE/BRDCAST
1697 Broadway, #602
New York, NY 10019 USA
212-489-6710
FAX: 212-307-6237

NASHVILLE FILM OFFICE
161 Fourth Avenue North
Nashville, TN 37219 USA
615-259-4777
FAX: 615-256-3074

NATCHEZ FILM COMMISSION
422 Main
P.O. Box 1485
Natchez, MS 39121 USA
601-446-6345
800-647-6724
FAX: 601-442-0814

NATIONAL FILM COMMISSION–
MEXICO
Atletas 2 Col. Country Club
Mexico City, D. F. 4220 MEXICO
525-549-2375
525-549-3060 x330
FAX: 525-549-2347

NAVAJO NATION FILM OFFICE
P.O. Box 2310
Window Rock, AZ 86515 USA
520-871-6655
FAX: 520-871-7355

NEBRASKA FILM OFFICE
700 South 16th
P.O. Box 94666
Lincoln, NE 68509-4666 USA
402-471-3680
800-228-4307
FAX: 402-471-3026

NEW HAMPSHIRE FILM & TV BUREAU
172 Pembroke Road
P.O. Box 1856
Concord, NH 03302-1856 USA
603-271-2598
FAX: 603-271-2629

NEW JERSEY MOTION PICTURE/TV
COMMISSION
153 Halsey Street
P.O. Box 47023
Newark, NJ 7101 USA
201-648-6279
FAX: 201-648-7350

NEW MEXICO FILM OFFICE
1100 South St. Francis Drive
P. O. Box 20003
Santa Fe, NM 87504-5003 USA
800-545-9871
505-827-9810
FAX: 505-827-9799

NEW ORLEANS FILM AND VIDEO
COMMISSION
1515 Poydras Street, Suite 1200
New Orleans, LA 70112 USA
504-565-8104
FAX: 504-565-8108

NEW SOUTH WALES FILM &
TELEVISION OFFICE
Level 6, 1 Francis Street
Sydney, NSW 2010 AUSTRALIA
61-2-9380-5599
FAX: 61-2-9360-1090

NEW YORK STATE GOVERNOR'S
OFFICE OF /MOTION PICTURE AND
TELEVISION-DEVELOPMENT
633 Third Avenue, 33rd Floor
New York, NY 10017 USA
212-803-2330
FAX: 212-803-2339

NEWFOUNDLAND – DEPT. OF ITT
P.O. Box 8700
St. John's, Newfoundland A1B 4J6
CANADA
709-729-0598
800-563-2299
FAX: 709-729-3208

NORTH CAROLINA FILM OFFCE
430 North Salisbury Street
Raleigh, NC 27611 USA
919-733-9900
800-232-9227
FAX: 919-715-0151

NORTH DAKOTA FILM COMMISSION
604 East Boulevard, 2nd Floor
Bismarck, ND 58505 USA
800-328-2871
701-328-2525
FAX: 701-328-4878

NORTHERN SCREEN COMMISSION
Studio 15 - Design Works - William St.
Felling, Gateshead, Tyne&Wear NE10 OJP
ENGLAND
44-191-469-1000
FAX: 44-191-469-7000

NORTHWEST FLORIDA/OKALOOSA
FILM COMM.
P.O. Box 609
P.O. Box 4097
Ft. Walton Beach, FL 32549-0609
800-322-3319
FAX: 904-651-7149

NOVA SCOTIA FILM DEV. CORP./
LOCATION SVC
1724 Granville Street
Halifax, NS B3J 1X5 CANADA
902-424-7177
FAX: 902-424-0617

OAHU FILM OFFICE
530 South King Street, Room 306
Honolulu, Oahu, HI 96813 USA
808-527-6108
FAX: 808-523-4242

OAKLAND FILM COMMISSION
1333 Broadway, 9th Floor
Oakland, CA 94612 USA
510-238-4734
FAX: 510-238-2227

OCALA/MARION COUNTY CHAMBER
OF COMMERCE
110 East Silver Springs Boulevard
Ocala, FL 34470 USA
352-629-8051
FAX: 352-629-7651

OHIO FILM COMMISSION
77 South High Street, 29th Floor
P.O. Box 1001
Columbus, OH 43216-1001 USA
614-466-2284
800-230-3523
FAX: 614-466-6744

OKANAGAN-SIMILKAMEEN FILM
COMMISSION
27-9015 Westside Road
Kelowna, BC V1Y 8B2 CANADA
604-769-1834
FAX: 604-769-1864

OKLAHOMA FILM OFFICE
440 South Houston, Suite 304
Tulsa, OK 74127-8945 USA
918-581-2660
800-766-3456
FAX: 918-581-2244

OMAHA FILM COMMISSION
6800 Mercy Road, Suite 202
Omaha, NE 68106-2627 USA
402-444-7736
402-444-7737
FAX: 402-444-4511

ONTARIO FILM DEVELOPMENT
CORPORATION
175 Bloor St. East, # 300, North Tower
Toronto, ONT M4W 3R8 CANADA
416-314-6858
FAX: 416-314-6876
213-960-4787
FAX: 213-960-4786

ORANGE COUNTY FILM COMMISSION
2 Park Plaza, Suite 100
Irvine, CA 92614 USA
714-476-2242
800-628-8033
FAX: 714-476-0513

OREGON FILM & VIDEO OFFICE
121 SW Salmon Street, Suite 300A
Portland, OR 97204 USA
503-229-5832
Shoot@Oregonfilm.org
FAX: 503-229-6869

PACIFIC FILM & TELEVISION
COMMISSION
GPO Box 1436
Brisbane, Queensland 4001 AUSTRALIA
617-3224-4114
FAX: 617-3224-6717

PAGE-LAKE POWELL FILM
COMMISSION
P.O. Box 727
Page, AZ 86040 USA
520-645-2741
FAX: 520-645-3181

PALM BEACH CTY FILM AND
TELEVISION COMM.
1555 Palm Beach Lakes Blvd., Suite 414
West Palm Beach, FL 33401 USA
561-233-1000
800-745-FILM
filmcomm@co.palm-beach.fl.us
FAX: 561-683-6957

PALM SPRINGS DESERT RESORTS
CVB/FILM OFF
69-930 Highway 111, Suite 201
Rancho Mirage, CA 92270 USA
619-770-9000
800-96-RESORTS
FAX: 619-770-9001

PARK CITY FILM COMMISSION
P.O. Box 1630
Park City, UT 84060 USA
801-649-6100
800-453-1360
FAX: 801-649-4132

PENNSYLVANIA FILM OFFICE
200 N. 3rd Street, Suite 901
Harrisburg, PA 17101 USA
717-783-3456
FAX: 717-772-3581

PITTSBURGH FILM OFFICE
Benedum Trees Building, Suite 1300
Pittsburgh, PA 15222 USA
412-261-2744
800-471-7335
FAX: 412-471-7317

PLACER COUNTY FILM OFFICE
13460 Lincoln Way, #A
Auburn, CA 95603 USA
916-887-2111
FAX: 916-887-2134

PRINCE EDWARD ISLAND FILM
OFFICE
c/o Enterprise PEI
P. O. Box 910
Charlottetown, PEI C1A 7L9 CANADA
902-368-6329
FAX: 902-368-6301

PROVIDENCE FILM COMMISSION
400 Westminster Street, 6th Floor
Providence, RI 02903 USA
401-273-3456
FAX: 401-274-8240

PUERTO RICO FILM COMMISSION
355 F.D. Roosevelt Ave/Fomento Bldg #106
San Juan, 00918 USA
809-758-4747
809-754-7110
FAX: 809-756-5706

QUAD CITIES DEV. GROUP/FILM
COALITION
1830 2nd Avenue, Suite 200
Rock Island, IL 61201 USA
309-326-1005
FAX: 309-788-4964

QUEBEC CITY FILM BUREAU
171 St.-Paul Street, Suite 100
Quebec City, QB G1K 3W2 CANADA
418-692-5338
FAX: 418-692-5602

REDDING/SHASTA COUNTY FILM
COMMISSION
777 Auditorium Drive
Redding, CA 96001 USA
916-225-4100
800-874-7562
FAX: 916-225-4354

RIDGECREST FILM COMMISSION
100 West California Avenue
Ridgecrest, CA 93555 USA
619-375-8202
800-847-4830
FAX: 619-371-1654

ROCHESTER/FINGER LAKES FILM/
VIDEO OFF.
126 Andrews Street
Rochester, NY 14604-1102 USA
716-546-5490
FAX: 716-232-4822

SACRAMENTO AREA FILM
COMMISSION
1421 K Street
Sacramento, CA 95814 USA
916-264-7777
FAX: 916-264-7788

SAINT LOUIS FILM OFFICE
330 North 15th Street
Saint Louis, MO 63103 USA
314-259-3409
FAX: 314-421-2489

SAN ANTONIO FILM COMMISSION
P.O. Box 2277
San Antonio, TX 78230 USA
210-270-8700
800-447-3372x730/777
FAX: 210-270-8782

SAN DIEGO FILM COMMISSION
402 West Broadway, Suite 1000
San Diego, CA 92101-3585 USA
619-234-3456
FAX: 619-234-0571

SAN FRANCISCO FILM & VIDEO ARTS
COMM.
Mayor's Office - 401 Van Ness Ave., #417
San Francisco, CA 94102 USA
415-554-6244
sffilmcomm@aol.com
FAX: 415-554-6503

SAN JOSE FILM & VIDEO
COMMISSION
333 West San Carlos, Suite #1000
San Jose, CA 95110 USA
408-295-9600
800-726-5673
FAX: 408-295-3937

SAN LUIS OBISPO COUNTY FILM
COMMISSION
1041 Chorro Street, Suite E
San Luis Obispo, CA 93401 USA
805-541-8000
FAX: 805-543-9498

SANTA CLARITA VLY. FILM &
TOURISM BUREAU
23920 Valencia Boulevard, Suite 125
Santa Clarita, CA 91355-2175 USA
800-4FILMSC
805-259-4787
FAX: 805-259-7304

SANTA CRUZ COUNTY CONF. & VIS.
COUNCIL
701 Front Street
Santa Cruz, CA 95060 USA
408-425-1234
FAX: 408-425-1260

SANTA MONICA MOUNTAINS NRA
30401 Agoura Road, Suite 100
Agoura Hills, CA 91301 USA
818-597-1036 ext 212
FAX: 818-597-8537

SASKFILM / LOCATIONS
SASKATCHEWAN
2445 - 13th Avenue, Suite 340
Regina, Saskatchewan S4P OW1 CANADA
306-347-3456
FAX: 306-359-7768

SAVANNAH FILM COMMISSION
P.O. Box 1027
Savannah, GA 31402 USA
912-651-3696
FAX: 912-238-0872

SCOTTISH SCREEN LOCATIONS
74 Victoria Crescent Road
Glasgow, G12 9JN SCOTLAND
44-141-339-1500
FAX: 44-141-339-7744

SCOTTSDALE FILM OFFICE
3939 Civic Center Boulevard
Scottsdale, AZ 85251 USA
602-994-2636
FAX: 602-994-7780

SEATTLE / MAYOR'S OFFICE OF FILM
& VIDEO
600 4th Avenue - 2nd Floor
Seattle, WA 98104 USA
206-684-5030
FAX: 206-684-5360

SEDONA FILM COMMISSION
P.O. Box 2489
Sedona, AZ 86339 USA
520-204-1123
FAX: 520-204-1064

SHREVEPORT-BOSSIER FILM
COMMISSION
P.O. Box 1761
Shreveport, LA 71166 USA
318-222-9391
800-551-8682
FAX: 318-222-0056

SONOMA COUNTY FILM LIAISON
OFFICE
5000 Roberts Lake Road, Suite A
Rohnert Park, CA 94928 USA
707-586-8100
707-586-8110
FAX: 707-586-8111

SOUTH AUSTRALIAN FILM
CORPORATION
3 Butler Drive, Hendon Common
Adelaide, South Australia 5014
AUSTRALIA
618-348-9300
FAX: 618-347-0385

SOUTH CAROLINA FILM OFFICE
P.O. Box 7367
Columbia, SC 29202 USA
803-737-0490
FAX: 803-737-3104

SOUTH DAKOTA FILM COMMISSION
711 East Wells Avenue
Pierre, SD 57501-3369 USA
605-773-3301
FAX: 605-773-3256

SOUTH WEST FILM COMMISSION
18 Bellevue Road
Saltash, Cornwall PL12 6TG UNITED
KINGDOM
44-1752-841199
FAX: 44-1752-841254

SOUTH WEST SHORE FILM
COMMISSION
P. O. Box 131
Yarmouth, Nova Scotia B5A 4B1 CANADA
902-742-3210
FAX: 902-742-3107

SOUTH OF FRANCE FILM
COMMISSION
Montee de Villeneuve
Entrecasteaux, Var 83570 FRANCE
33-04-94-04-4070
FAX: 33-04-94-04-4998
Saint Tropez Bureau:
33-94-54-8188 FAX: 33-94-97-7606

SOUTHEASTERN CONNECTICUT FILM
OFFICE
PO Box 89
New London, CT 06320-4974 USA
800-657-FILM
860-444-2206
FAX: 860-442-4257

SOUTHWEST FLORIDA FILM
COMMISSION
Beverly Fox / Beverley Dale
24840 Burnt Pine Drive, Suite 1
Bonita Springs, FL 34134 USA
941-498-5498
FAX: 941-498-5497

SPACE COAST FILM COMMISSION
c/o Brevard Cty Gvt Ctr, 2725 St. Johns
Melbourne, FL 32940 USA
407-633-2110
800-93-OCEAN
FAX: 407-633-2112

SRI LANKA FILM COMMISSION
5699 Kanan Road, Suite 319
Agoura Hills, CA 91301 USA
310-201-8448
FAX: 805-496-4840

TAMPA FILM COMMISSION
111 E. Madison Street, Suite 1010
Tampa, FL 33602-4706 USA
813-223-1111 x58
FAX: 813-229-6616

TEMECULA VALLEY FILM COUNCIL
P. O. Box 1786
Temecula, CA 92593 USA
909-699-6267
FAX: 909-694-1999

TENNESSEE FILM/ENTERTAINMNT/
MUSIC COMM.
320 6th Avenue North, 7th Floor
Nashville, TN 37243-0790 USA
615-741-3456
800-251-8594
FAX: 615-741-5829

TEXAS FILM COMMISSION
P.O. Box 13246
Austin, TX 78711 USA
512-463-9200
FAX: 512-463-4114

THAILAND FILM PROMOTION
CENTER
599 Bumrung Muang Road
Bangkok, 10100 THAILAND
66-2-223-4690
66-2-223-4474
FAX: 66-2-223-2586

THE CITY OF LIVERPOOL FILM
OFFICE
William Brown Street, Central Libraries
Liverpool, L3 8EW ENGLAND
44-151-225-5446
FAX: 44-151-207-1342

THE INLAND EMPIRE FILM
COMMISSION
301 E. Vanderbilt Way, Suite 100
San Bernardino, CA 92408 USA
909-890-1090
800-500-4367
FAX: 909-890-1088

THE MAINE FILM OFFICE
State House Station 59
Augusta, ME 04333-0059 USA
207-287-5703
FAX: 207-287-8070
(E-mail: gregory.d.gadberry@state.me.us)

THOMPSON-NICOLA FILM
COMMISSION
2079 Falcon Road
Kamloops, BC V2C 4J2 CANADA
604-372-9336
FAX: 604-372-5048

TORONTO FILM AND TELEVISION
OFFICE
2nd Floor, West Tower, New City Hall
Toronto, ONT M5H 2N2 CANADA
416-392-7570
FAX: 416-392-0675

TRINIDAD FILM COMMISSION
136 West Main Street
Trinidad, CO 81082 USA
719-846-9412
800-748-1970
FAX: 719-846-4550

TUCSON FILM OFFICE
32 North Stone Avenue, Suite 100
Tucson, AZ 85701 USA
520-791-4000
520-429-1000
FAX: 520-791-4963

TUOLUMNE COUNTY FILM
COMMISSION
P. O. Box 4020
Sonora, CA 95370 USA
209-533-4420
800-446-1333
kelli@mlode.com
FAX: 209-533-0956

TUPELO FILM COMMISSION
P.O. Box 1485
Tupelo, MS 38802-1485 USA
601-841-6454
800-533-0611
FAX: 601-841-6558

U.S. VIRGIN ISLANDS FILM
PROMOTION OFF.
P.O. Box 6400
St. Thomas, V.I. 804 USVI
809-775-1444
809-774-8784
FAX: 809-774-4390

UTAH FILM COMMISSION
324 South State, Suite 500
Salt Lake City, UT 84114-7330 USA
801-538-8740
800-453-8824
FAX: 801-538-8886

UTAH'S SOUTHWEST FILM
COMMISSION
906 N. 1400 West
St. George, UT 84770 USA
801-628-4171
800-233-8824
FAX: 801-673-3540

VALLEJO/SOLANO COUNTY FILM
COMMISSION
495 Mare Island Way
Vallejo, CA 94590 USA
707-642-3653
800-4-VALLEJO
FAX: 707-644-2206

VENEZUELA FILM COMMISSION
Av.Diego Cisneros,Centro Colgate,Ala
Sur,Piso 2,LR
Caracas, 70102 VENEZUELA
58-2-238-89-26
58-2-237-49-42
FAX: 58-2-238-52-30

VICTORIA/VANCOUVER ISLAND FILM
COMM.
525 Fort Street
Victoria, BC V8W 1E8 CANADA
604-386-3976
FAX: 604-385-3552

VIRGINIA FILM OFFICE
901 East Byrd St., 19th Flr. (Zip 23219)
P.O. Box 798
Richmond, VA 23206-0798 USA
804-371-8204
800-641-0810 (Info)
vafilm@vedp.state.va.us
FAX: 804-371-8177

VOLUSIA COUNTY FILM OFFICE
123 E. Orange Avenue
P.O. Box 910
Daytona Beach, FL 32114 USA
904-255-0415
800-544-0415
FAX: 904-255-5478

WASHINGTON STATE FILM OFFICE
2001 6th Avenue, Suite 2600
Seattle, WA 98121 USA
206-464-7148
FAX: 206-464-7222

WEST VIRGINIA FILM OFFICE
State Capital, Building 6, Room 525
Charleston, WV 25305-0311 USA
304-558-2234
800-982-3386
FAX: 304-558-1189

WESTERN NORTH CAROLINA FILM
COMMISSION
P.O. Box 1258
Arden, NC 28704 USA
704-687-7234
FAX: 704-687-7552

WICHITA CONVENTION & VISITORS
BUREAU
100 South Main, Suite 100
Wichita, KS 67202 USA
316-265-2800
800-288-9424
FAX: 316-265-0162

WICKENBURG FILM COMMISSION
216 North Frontier Street
P.O. Drawer CC
Wickenburg, AZ 85358 USA
520-684-5479
FAX: 520-684-5470

WILMINGTON REGIONAL FILM
COMMISSION
#1 Estell Lee Place
Wilmington, NC 28401 USA
910-763-0847
FAX: 910-762-9765

WINSTON-SALEM PIEDMONT TRIAD
FILM COMM.
601 West Fourth Street
Winston-Salem, NC 27101 USA
910-777-3787 x7
wsflmoff@aol.com
FAX: 910-721-2209

WISCONSIN FILM OFFICE
123 West Washington Avenue, 6th Floor
Madison, WI 53702-0001 USA
608-267-3456
800-345-6947
FAX: 608-266-3403

WYOMING FILM OFFICE
I-25 and College Drive
Cheyenne, WY 82002-0240 USA
307-777-3400
800-458-6657
FAX: 307-777-6904

YAMPA VALLEY FILM BOARD, INC
Box 772305
Steamboat Springs, CO 80477 USA
970-879-0882
FAX: 970-879-2543

YELLOWKNIFE ECON. DEV. AUTH. &
FILM COM.
Box 1688
Yellowknife, NT X1A 2P3 CANADA
403-873-5772
FAX: 403-920-5649

YORKSHIRE SCREEN COMMISSION
The Workstation, 15 Paternoster Row
Sheffield, Yorkshire S1 2BX UNITED
KINGDOM
44-1142-799-115
44-1142-796-811
FAX: 44-1142-798-593
FAX: 44-1142-796-522

YUKON FILM COMMISSON
P.O. Box 2703
Whitehorse, Yukon Y1A 2C6 CANADA
403-667-5400
FAX: 403-393-6456

YUMA FILM COMMISSION
2557 Arizona Avenue, Suite A
Yuma, AZ 85364 USA
520-341-1616
520-726-4027
FAX: 520-341-1685

GLOSSARY

Action. Mental or physical motion needed to reach a goal.

Additive Color. Mix of basic colors.

Ambiant. Natural, environmental sound.

Angle. The point of view (POV) of the camera when it is set up for shooting.

Antagonist. Villain.

Apex (Scene). Characters operating from equal dominance levels.

Arc. Hard beam of light.

Back Story. An incident that occures prior to Act I.

Background. Does not illuminate subjects / objects.

Barn Door. Attachment on a light fixture, used to direct beam of light.

Base. Minimum amount of light needed to have camera operate properly.

Basic. Consists of key light, backlight, fill light.

Camera Movements. The PANning, tilting or tracking of a motion picture camera.

Character. The person an actor is portraying in a production.

Choreography. Actors' movements within a scene.

Color Temperature. Color consistency.

Complex. A character showing several traits which may be complementary or contradictory.

Continuity. Stresses the facts to be shown.

Depth of Field. The range of acceptable sharpness.

Diffused. Illuminates a large area with indistinct light beams.

Directing Style. The director's individual visual technique selected to symbolize human emotions and actions in the film.

Directional. Illuminates small area with distinct light beam.

Disjunctive. Explains a character's emotions in a subliminal way.

Distortion. Increased or decreased volume.

Dolly. Movement in or away from subject / object.

Dynamic. Conveys meaning.

Editing. The process of selecting, arranging and assembling a film and its sound track into a logical, rhythmical story progression.

Effective Memory. When an actor relives a personal, highly emotional event.

Empathetic. Relies on contrast.

Emphasis. Special attention or effort directed toward visual, emotional or physical traits.

Environment. Unifies location and narrative.

Epic. Relies upon panoramic sweep of setting and characters.

Expressive. Goes far beyond realism.

Facts/Assumptions. Drawing one's conclusions from the given facts of what a character does .or says about himself and / or what others say about him

Flat. No characteristics; usually episodic player, (i.e., taxi driver, sales clerk).

Forward Movement. Scenes moving story / plot line along.

Hard. Casts shadows.

High Angle. Camera is placed high in relation to eyeline.

High Key. Frame is well-lit.

Incandescent. The amount of light falling on a scene.

Invisible. Depends on primary and secondary movements.

Kicker. Illuminates one side of an actor's face.

Lighting Plot. A blueprint for arranging the placement of lights and accompanying equipment.

Light. The illumination of a scene to achieve a desired mood or atmosphere in a photographic image.

Line of Action. A character's goal leading to his actions.

Lineament. A character's build, posture.

Low Angle. Camera is placed low in relation to eyeline.

Low Key. Light cutting through shadows.

Method. Acting style originated by Stanislawski (Moscow Art Theater) and perfected by American acting coach / actor Lee Strasberg.

Motivated. Identifies environment (street light).

Nagra. Recording machine.

Narrative. A film's plot.

Omnipotent. The viewer sees everything and knows everything.

Overlapping. No transmission is used from one sound to the other; sounds overlap.

Pace. A character's emotional intensity.

PAN. Camera follows subject's / object's primary movement.

Physical. Stresses physical actions.

Physicalization. The actor expresses his goals and / or emotions via physical actions.

Picturalization. Camera framing.

Plot Point. An event intensifying goal and / or obstacle.

Plot. Same as narrative, a film's story line.

Primary. A character's traits.

Primary. Camera is static.

Rack Focus. Throws either background or foreground out of focus.

Realistic. Presents an unbroken illusion of reality.

Release Object. The actor igniting emotions via the senses of Sight, Sound, Hearing, Taste, Smell.

Rhythm. An event that affects the character's physical reaction.

Rim. Adds a rim of light around subject/object.

Scene Breakdown. List of a scene's requirements as to actors needed, props, costumes, sound, etc.

Scrim. A veil placed over light fixture.

Secondary. Camera moves.

Secondary. The way a character reacts to environment.

Segue. One sound fades out, another sound fades in.

Sense Memory. Segment of Method Acting.

Sense of Being. A character's emotional and physical state.

Separate. Creates counterpoint to the visual image.

Shooting Schedule. Timetable of principal photography.

Shot List. List of a scene's camera setups.

Simple. A single Character Trait dominating a character.

Soft. A scrim is placed over the light fixture.

Soft. Illuminates an entire area.

Sound loops. A length of tape spliced into a loop.

Sound Sequencing. Choosing of sound segments and which type of transitions should be used between them.

Sound. The audio portion of a film that is recorded on magnetic tape or magnetic film.

Storyboard. Pictoral depiction of a scene's choreography.

Straight Cut. Cut from sound to sound (dialogue).

Subjective. Sets the motive needed in order to have viewer wonder about suspense levels.

Subjective. The viewer is in the hero's shoes.

Substitution. The actor's use of Sense Memory in lieu of personally experienced emotions.

Survey PAN. Camera looks over an entire area without specific point of interest.

Target. Points of attention (actor, another actor, what is thought of or spoken about).

Tertiary. A shot taken by two or more cameras.

Tilt. Camera moves up or down.

Timing. Computerized color correction.

Tracking PAN. Bisects the subject's/object's movement.

Twist. An event that turns the story around.

Viewpoint. The position the director wishes the viewer to take.

Visual. Stresses visual aspects.

Whip PAN. Extremely fast pan.

Zinger. Extremely hard light.

Zoom. Camera rapidly moves toward or away from subject/object.

BIBLIOGRAPHY

Seger, Linda. Making A Good Script Great. Hollywood: Samuel French

Seger, Linda. Creating Unforgettable Characters. Hollywood: Samuel French

Hunter, Lew. Screenwriting 434. New York: Perigree Books/Putnam Pubishing Group

Harmon, Renée. The Beginning Filmmaker's Guide To Directing. New York: Renée Harmon Walker and Company

Harmon, Renée. The Beginning Filmmaker's Business Guide. New York: Renée Harmon Walker and Company

Harmon, Renée. Film Producing—Low Budget Films That Sell. Hollywood: Samuel French

Katz, Steven D. Cinematic Motion—A Workshop For Staging Scenes. Hollywood: Michael Wiese Productions

Wiese, Michael. Film And Video Financing. Hollywood: Michael Wiese Productions

Wiese, Michael. Film And Video Marketing. Hollywood: Michael Wiese Productions

Singleton, Ralph. Film Budgeting. Los Angeles: Lone Eagle Publishing Co.

Singleton, Ralph. Film Scheduling. Los Angeles: Lone Eagle Publishing Co.

Singleton, Ralph. Film Scheduling/Film Budgeting Workbook. Los Angeles: Lone Eagle Publishing Co.

Singleton, Ralph. Movie Production & Budget Forms. Los Angeles: Lone Eagle Publishing Co.

INDEX

A

Accoutrements   56, 59
Act I   20, 39, 40, 41
Act II   20, 39, 40, 41
Act II   20, 41
Ambient Sound   94
American Society Of Composers,
    Authors And Publishers
    ASCAP   100
Apex   23
Art Director, *see* Production
    Designer
Arthur   60
ASCAP, *see* American Society Of
    Composers, Authors And
    Publishers

B

Balance   76
Birds, The   14
Breakfast At Tiffanys   49
Brest, Martin   21

C

Camera Framing
    Balance   76
    Symmetry   76
Camera Lenses   70, 71
    Standard   71
    Telephoto   71
    Wide Angle   71
Camera Movement   65, 70

Camera Viewpoint   73
    Close Up   74
        Extreme   75
    High Angle   73
    Low Angle   74
Campbell, Martin   50
Canting Viewpoint   73
Change Of Speed   84
Changing Rhythms   19
Character
    Clothing   59
    Getting To Know   42
    High Person   23
    Low Person   23
    Movement   65
    Place   57
    Time Of Day   59
Character Trait
    Complementary   49, 50
    Contradictory   49, 51, 55
    Dominant   48, 49, 50, 51, 55, 56
Characters
    Complex   48, 50, 53
    Dominant Character Trait   49, 50
    Dominant Trait   55, 56
    Flat   48
    Lineament   48, 49, 50
    Simple   48, 49, 56
Charisma   121
Cimino, Michael   13
Cinematographer   3, 5
    Duties Of   5
Close Up   74
    Viewpoint   73
Clothing For Characters   59

Communication
  Levels Of   22, 23, 24
Complementary Angles   82
Conflict   12, 35, 36
  In Forward Movement   35
  Man Versus Himself   36
  Man Versus Man   36
  Man Versus Nature   36
Continuity Editing   85, 87
Coppola, Francis Ford   13
Crossfade   98
Cut In   83
Cut Out   83
Cutting Your Film
  Guidelines   82

D

Dean, James   121
Dead Man Walking   36, 56
Deer Hunter, The   13
Depth Of Field   71
DGA
  see Directors Guild Of America
Dialogue
  Recorded   96
Directing
  Style   11
    Epic   12
    Expressive   13
    Realistic   11
    Visual Technique   11
Directional Continuity   82
Director
  Collaboration
    With Editor   6
    With Producer   3
    With Production Designer   6
    With Production Manager   4
    With Writer   4, 10
  Duties Of   10
  Responsibility Of   2

Director Of Photography (DP)
  see Cinematographer
Director's Guild Of America
  (DGA)   8
  Contract   8
Disjunctive Sound   96
Dog Day Afternoon   24
Dolly Shot   67, 69, 70
  In   69, 70, 80
  Out   69
Dominance Pattern, Shifting   23
Down Tilt   69
DP, *see* Cinematographer
Dynamic Editing   85, 87

E

Editing   78
  Change Of Speed   84
  Complementary Angles   82
  Cut In   83
  Cut Out   83
  Directional Continuity   82
  Jump Cut   83
  Master Shot   81
  Neutral Shot   82
  Parallel Cutting   83
  Sound   98
Editing Concepts   11, 85
  Continuity   85, 87
  Dynamic   85, 87
  Emphatic   87, 89
  Invisible Editing   11, 86
  Point Of View   85
  Sound   94
Editor   3, 6
  Duties Of   6
Edwards, Blake   49
Effective Memory   124
Emotional Emphasis In Omnipotent
    Viewpoint   29
Emotions   18

Emphasis
  Emotional   29, 31
  Physical   29, 32
  Visual   29, 30
English Patient, The   56
Environment
  Impacting Choice Of Directing
    Style   10, 15, 56
Environment   15
Epic Style Of Directing   12
Exorcist, The   14
Expressive Style Of Directing   13
Extreme Close Up   75
Eyelines   80, 81

F

Film, Changing Rhythms   19
Filmgoers Companion, The   78
Footage Counters   99
Forward Movement   35
Framing   64, 76
  Balance   76
  Symmetry   76
Friedkin, William   14

G

Garland, Judy   121
Getting To Know Characters   42
Gettysburg   36, 77
Godfather, The   13
Goldeneye   49
Gradation Of Rhythm And Pacing
    17
Gramercy Pictures   50
Griffith, D.W.   78
Grumpy Old Men   50

H

Halliwell, Leslie   78
Herek, Stephen   96
High Angle Viewpoint   73

Highlight Sequence   41
Hitchcock, Alfred   14

I

Intensity Level   17, 20, 21
Intensity Level I   17, 18, 19, 20
Intensity Level II   17, 18, 19, 20
Intensity Level III   17, 18, 19, 20
Intensity Pattern
  Changing   19
Intercutting   83
Investment Contract   3

J

Julian, Rupert   74
Jump Cut   83

L

Lenses
  Camera   70, 71
  Depth Of Field   71
Letter Of Intent   3
Lighting   76
Limited Partnership   3
Logical Cinematic Interpretation   4
Loop   98
Low Angle   74
  Viewpoint   73, 74
Lumet, Sidney   24

M

Manghella, Anthony   56
Marshall, Gary   12
Master Shot   81
Maxwell, Ronald F.   77
MCA   12, 13, 14, 21
Memory, Effective   124
MGM   24, 50
Midnight Cowboy   24
Miramax Films   50

Mixing Session   99
Mixing Sound   99
Monroe, Marilyn   121
Motive   4, 79
Movement   65
   Camera   65, 70
   Character   65
   Primary   65
   Secondary   65, 67, 78, 85
   Tertiary   65, 70
Moving The Story Forward   35, 40
Mr. Holland's Opus   96
Music   50, 94, 100

N

Need   35
   In Forward Movement   35
Neutral Shot   82

O

Omnipotent Viewpoint   27
Overlapping Sound   95

P

Pacing   10, 17, 18, 21
Pakula, Alan J.   21
Panoramic Use Of Setting And
   Action   12
   see also Epic Style Of Directing
Parallel Cutting   83
Paramount   13, 49
Pelican Brief, The   21
Petrie, Donald   50
Phantom Of The Opera, The   74
Physical Condition   59
Physical Emphasis, In Omnipotent
   Viewpoint   29
Place, Regarding Characters   57
Point Of View Editing   85
Presley, Elvis   121

Pretty Woman   12
Primary Sense Of Being   56
Producer   2, 3
   Duties Of   3
Production Designer   3, 6
   Duties Of   6
Production Manager   2, 4
   Duties Of   4
Psycho   14

R

Reaction   4
Realistic Style Of Directing   11
Recorded Dialogue   96
Rhythm   10, 17, 18
Rhythm And Pacing, Gradation
   17
Robbins, Tim   56

S

Scene, Place   57
Scent Of A Woman   21
Schindlers List   12, 56
Schlesinger, John   24
Script
   Analysis   10
   Shooting   6, 10, 16, 17,
      27, 29, 80, 84, 90, 91
Secondary Sense Of Being   56
Segue   98
Sense Memories   124
Sense Of Being
   Primary   56
   Secondary   56
Separate Sound   95
Sequence
   Highlight   41
Shifting Viewpoint, *see* Omnipotent
   Viewpoint
Shooting Script   6, 10, 16, 17,
      27, 29, 80, 84, 90, 91

Shot
  Dolly
    In 69, 70, 80
    Out 69
  Master 81
  Tilt 67, 69
    Down 69
    Up 69
  Zoom 70
Sound 50, 93, 94, 95, 96, 97, 98, 99
  Ambient 94
  Correction 98
  Disjunctive 96
  Editing 98
  Footage Counters 99
  Mixing 99
  Music 100
  Overlapping 95
  Recorded Dialogue 96
  Selection 98
  Separate 95
  Sequencing 98
    Crossfade 98
    Loop 98
    Segue 98
    Straight Cut 98
  Start Marks 99
  Voice Distortion 95
Sound, Dialogue And Music 94
Sound Editing 97
Sound Of Music, The 50
Spielberg, Steven 12, 50
Standard Lens 71
Stars Charisma 121
Start Marks 99
Straight Cut 98
Structure 36, 39
Style Of Directing
  Epic 12, 13
  Expressive 13, 14
Subjective Patterns Of Realism 13
  see also Expressive Style Of
    Directing
Subjective Viewpoint 27
Survey Pan 68

Suspense 35, 37, 38
  In Forward Movement 35
Symmetry 76

T

Teamwork 2
Telephoto Lens 71
Tertiary Movement 70
Tilt Shot 67, 69
  Down Tilt 69
  Up Tilt 69
Time Of Day Regarding
    Characters 59
Touchstone 12, 96
Tracking Pan 68
Turner Pictures 77

U

Unbroken Illusion Of Reality 11
  see also Realistic Style
    Of Directing
Universal 50
Up Tilt 69

V

Viewpoint 27, 28, 29, 64, 73, 74
  Canting 73
  Close Up 73, 74
    Extreme 75
  High Angle 73
  Low Angle 73, 74
  Normal 73
  Omnipotent 27
  Subjective 27, 28, 29
Visual Emphasis 29, 30
  In Omnipotent Viewpoint 29
Voice Distortion 95

W

Warner Bros.   14, 21, 24, 41, 50
Whip Pan   68
Wide Angle Lens   71
Wise, Robert   50
Writer   2, 4
   Duties Of   4

Z

Zoom   67, 70
   Shot   67, 70

ABOUT THE AUTHOR

Renée Harmon is a professional actress, scriptwriter, director, producer and president of her own production company. She has twelve feature films in theatrical and/or home video distribution. Harmon has lectured on motion pictures and for more than fifteen years has taught workshops at several California colleges. She is the author of ten successful books on making it in the movie business.